ZINDABAD!

Supporting Education Leaders
from Accra to Taipei

RAPHAEL WILKINS

Acknowledgements

I am grateful to the people and organisations who enabled these trips to happen, to the colleagues who came with me, to local hosts, friends and guides for enriching the experience, to my late wife Mary for tolerating my absences, to my daughter Kathryn for her encouragement and support, and especially to Michelle Emerson for her professional support with editing and publication.

Contents

Chapter One

Lahore: First Step on a New Journey

August Bank Holiday Monday, 2012. Gatwick Airport's North Terminal. Here I am, this is me: the shy-looking guy in a black suit with a briefcase. Early, because I came last night and stayed in a hotel. Sitting waiting for my colleague Ian. It will be the first time we have done a trip together. We are going to Lahore, capital of Punjab Province, Pakistan. I'll be there two weeks, then a bit later I'll be off to Karachi, then to Gujerat in India, then to all sorts of places I won't know about until nearer the time. It's work, of course - I couldn't travel like this otherwise - but there is always leisure time to soak up sights, flavours, culture. Why not come with me? Go on, pack your bag (in your mind's eye!) and keep me company. I'll tell you more about myself, but most of that had best wait until we're airborne in case you change your mind.

The bit I need to tell you now, otherwise I can't explain how I am using this waiting time, is that I am an educationist. Yes, that's right: studious, short-sighted, didactic, uptight, formal, never really learnt how to relate to other adults. You've got the picture straight away. The thing is, I can't shake off my preference for educational year diaries, the ones that end in August. So in August I transfer information from the old to the new, like most people do in January. Or used to do, when diaries had real paper pages. It's a good task for filling time and staying unobtrusive in an airport terminal. I am puzzling over what to do about a certain piece of information: a list that is important to me. Opportunities to travel to faraway places as part of my educational work began totally unexpectedly in 2007. I never thought they would continue. By the end of the academic year 2009-10 I had completed 17 international consultancy trips. I had been keeping a list in my diary, and copied it into my new diary for 2010-11. By the end of 2010-11 the total had grown to 25. In 2011-12, I added a further ten to the same list, to save the bother of writing it out afresh.

This is not just a boyish glee in collecting. When a client asks, 'How many times have you visited my country?' or 'Which countries have you worked in most?', or 'When were you last here?', it does not give a business-like impression to say, 'I don't know, I can't remember'.

I am about to start trip number 36. What shall I do about the list? It is getting unwieldy. Reluctantly I decide it is time to take the obvious step of putting it on computer. Out comes my laptop; I set about the task. In the pocket diary, this had been simply a list of towns. Now, it seems sensible to jot a few words of description, the actual dates, the client, and other brief comments to help my memory. That is how Ian finds me. I save the file and give him my attention.

Ian is taller than me, older than me, more successful than me, more confident than me. I am his boss for this trip. That's fine: we both have plenty of experience of taking different team roles according to the task. We exchange pleasantries, and board our flight which takes off at 10.00 am. It is due to land in Dubai at 7.50 pm, where we will have two hours before our next flight, which will get us to Lahore at 1.50 am on Tuesday.

Airborne, scrunched into economy, getting good views of Surrey and Sussex as the plane curves into alignment with the correct bearing for the flight, I am thinking, *so here I go again!* Not bad for a kid from a council estate who grew up without a father. But then not so good, either. This globetrotting phase wouldn't have happened if I hadn't crashed out of my main career at the age of 49. People got fed up with me, but if it hadn't been that year, that organisation, it would have been another. Some of us just don't mesh easily into organisations. Some of us prefer to keep ownership of our personalities and lifestyles.

All this travelling isn't actually taking me to a greater, meaningful destination. It takes me to the places themselves, of course. That is a joy, a privilege, a luxury which I soak up and relish with every pore. And I get to meet people in other cultural contexts, many of whom are interesting, and some truly inspiring. When it began, I hoped a new career phase would blossom, leading to professional success and recognition. I kept thinking that a big achievement might be just around the corner. Another hard push and a lucky break... Then earlier this summer I had been given a delightful taste of South America. Trips to Colombia, Brazil and Chile, oozing with spectacular scenery, rich culture and human warmth.

In Valparaiso I had the flash of self-knowledge that I had peaked professionally, and that the way forward would be a downward slide towards retirement. Even leaving aside the 'damaged goods' sticker that some potential business associates see on my forehead, how many people are able suddenly to achieve advancement in late career? Drinking in my first sight of the Pacific Ocean, I had known at that moment that having the chance to work globally was my high point, and the travel itself the only and best reward.

So here I go again, having just turned 61, heading towards a project which I had started earlier in the year. It is interesting and dead-centre to my expertise but is unlikely to proceed as planned. Duty and pride will ensure I take it as far as possible. The local organisers insisted on two full weeks of fieldwork, as so often over-estimating the time it takes an experienced consultant to understand a situation, so I predict there will be some dead time.

But right now, flying to Dubai is a drag because when I look at the map of the world in my head, I always underestimate how far east it is. Ian is happy to chat. He is widely travelled, but this will be his first visit to Pakistan. It is my seventh, spanning two very different projects. This one feels like a serious job of work. By comparison, the other feels like a pleasant holiday with friends. My previous visits have all been during the autumn and spring. This is my first in the monsoon season.

I have never been to Dubai the place. I only know Dubai the airport. What I mean is that I have never been to the place at ground level, to feel the warmth and breeze, the sand and sea or wander its opulent urban scene. Of course I have had the aerial view of the palm-shaped hotel built out into turquoise water and impossibly tall slender skyscrapers. The terminal buildings are a reassuring mooring. Marble, glass and chrome, palm trees and escalators, people like ants in cavernous spaces, refreshments from familiar outlets, then off again into the night. There is something distinctive about the atmosphere and mood of a flight from the Middle East to Pakistan on which the majority of the passengers are going home.

We land at Lahore and enter the terminal a bit after 2.00 am. The daytime scrum has long finished, so we edge forward quite quickly through the zealous formalities. The staff make sure that every new visitor's first impression of Pakistan is of military smartness. Then the real moment of arrival, walking out of the terminal and being hit by heat and humidity. The air is thick and soft and smells slightly of overblown roses.

The hotel has sent a minibus to meet the flight. We are the only passengers. I am so glad we are staying at the Avari Hotel because it is a known safe space, a mooring, a roost, as well as being very comfortable. My other project in Pakistan, the one that got me here in the first place, the one I am working on after this, is generously supported by Mr Avari, the owner of the hotel chain. He gives me and members of my team free accommodation in Karachi and here in Lahore, but that support is specific to that particular project.

The project we are working on now is funded and directed overall by the World Bank and project managed by one of the big project management companies. I'll just call it 'the company' if you don't mind. The client and beneficiary is the Schools Education Department of the Government of Punjab. A couple of sub-units are involved: the Directorate of Staff Development (DSD) and the Programme Monitoring and Implementation Unit (PMIU), which rub along somewhat awkwardly. The project spans a whole raft of ambitious activities intended to improve schools, only one of which concerns us. The organisation that Ian and I work for, which is a university, is providing the technical support for a strand of activity to professionalise the teaching workforce by advising on how to set up a Punjab Teachers

Standards and Development Authority as an autonomous body. If that set-up sounds like a recipe for a complicated muddle, you've got it spot on.

I came here back in the spring to assess the starting point and to propose a way forward. On that occasion, the company insisted on lodging me in a cheap, inconvenient hotel. Someone locally tipped me off that they were pulling a fast one, that in future, I should stick out for the Avari. In the run-up to this trip, I explained my situation to Mr Avari and asked if the cost could come within the range the company might regard as acceptable. The final details were sorted out between him and the young man in my office who handles the business side of things. That was funny because my assistant kept me posted with those exchanges, referring to Mr Avari by his first name as if he assumed he was dealing chummily with the booking clerk in Lahore.

We glide along through the night on the wide, straight, near-empty road from the airport to the city. There are no checkpoints today. Then into the confusing maze of city streets to the hotel's security barrier, and the grand entrance. All is dark and deserted except for one doorman and a desk clerk who sits bathed in a pool of orange light in the great shadowy interior, like a figure in a painting by a Dutch master. Our registrations are sorted, a porter appears. It takes me a little while to settle into a hotel room, to drink tea and unpack essentials. I am in bed by 4.30 am.

We meet at 9.00 am for breakfast. I pile my plate up with pooris and vegetables, which I would do anyway, but my previous experience of working with this client was of very late lunches, of variable quality. Ian is much more restrained. The hotel's comfortable lounge and eating area are bustling with morning activity. The doormen are in their colourful daytime uniforms with tall headdresses. In my room I send an email home, then at 10.00 am we start work.

A driver sent by the company is waiting for us in the foyer. He leads us through the front door to the car. The air outside reminds me of a steam room I sat in, in a spa in a hotel in Nairobi. This is our first view of the garden in daylight. It is as pristine as I remember, but the rows of flowers in pots won't need watering for quite a while. The company maintains an office which is a short drive away. I assume it is there mainly to impress clients because it is always virtually empty when I see it. Rosemary is waiting for us. She is our minder. That is my shorthand way of saying that she is a freelance consultant working with the company; she acts as the interface between us and the company; and the interface between the company and the bits of government we work with, and she escorts us to all significant work meetings. Rosemary has based herself in Pakistan for many years, she is towards the end of her career, and is a shrewd, careful survivor who doesn't say a lot.

I am looking forward to seeing the programme of events arranged for us. According to the agreed specification for this visit, we will be taken to representative districts and schools and engage in consultations with groups of stakeholders. So I am assuming we will get out and about, and see some different places in the varied landscape of Punjab.

Rosemary takes us to the office manager so that Ian can be formally introduced. She addresses the office manager as 'Colonel Sahib'. The colonel (retired) has a fair bit to say about the current security situation in the city, and about the drivers who will be looking after us. He explains that dengue is rife: it is common during the monsoon but particularly heavy this year. We should keep clear of stagnant water and minimise encounters with mosquitoes. He issues us with a mobile phone which will work locally. I give it to Ian, who is more adept - I would struggle to know which button to press to take a call.

We move to a quiet area to discuss the project. A quiet area is easy to find. It involves our choosing our favourite corner of the completely deserted open-plan office on the first floor. Our catch-up session is also quite straightforward in one way. Rosemary explains that nothing has happened since I was last here, and there is no programme, nor any arrangements made, for these two weeks of intensive consultancy, which has been in the diary for the last four months. Now this is interesting given that the company takes a sizeable fee for the detailed project management of the whole operation. I notice the slightest shadow of disquiet pass across Ian's otherwise impassive features.

Thus briefed, the three of us set off by car to visit the part of the government most centrally concerned with our project, which is the Directorate of Staff Development (DSD). It is housed in a neatly kept,

6

functional concrete block, painted white some years ago. When I was here previously, the only people I ever met were the director, Nadeem, and his two deputies, and the meetings were always in an impersonal meeting room off the vestibule, which did not involve actually going into the Directorate itself. I have worked with enough organisations to sense when I am being kept at arm's length and hidden from view.

Today we are shown into the same meeting room. Nadeem is all smiles and courtesy. He is flanked by his two deputies, who remain largely silent. He runs over what we all know already: that the purpose of the project is to set up a new autonomous body for the registration, licensing and certification of teachers. Then he sets out what he wants. There is no need to create an entirely new body. His Directorate can become that new body. It can be given autonomy and all the new powers it would need. So what he wants is for me to draft the legislation that will make that happen. I raise the question of how best to start gaining support for the teacher professionalisation process, knowing that it is opposed by the politically powerful teachers' unions and that there is as yet no shared vision of what it will look like and how it will work. Nadeem advises that it would be best if we don't tell anyone about these plans so that all the resistance can be saved up and dealt with in one big confrontation.

Which is not going to happen any time soon, I say to myself privately, as we go back to the Avari Hotel for a late lunch. Nadeem is a clever and thoughtful man. I have no doubt that he sees the brashness and haste of Western-designed intervention strategies, and makes his own judgements about how similar outcomes might be achieved better over a longer timescale and with more local ownership.

We drive through a short, very heavy shower of rain. The road is buzzing with a variety of traffic, including many light motorcycles. These usually carry two or three people, the women balanced side-saddle in light clothing, no-one wearing helmets. Sometimes the one driving the motorcycle is holding a phone in one hand and texting, and smoking a cigarette, at the same time as weaving in and out of horse and donkey carts, motorised rickshaws and cars. When a heavy downpour occurs, bridges and underpasses become packed with riders sheltering. We pass stationary donkey carts selling roasted corn cobs, which give off a pleasant barbecue smell, and fruit carts. The rain washes away the traffic fumes from the fruit.

Over lunch we talk through how best to adjust our work to take account of the morning's news. Did Rosemary know all along? I think it likely. We go back to DSD, as had been planned, for a detailed working session with the two deputies. In the course of our work, they tell us Michael is coming to town.

Michael is a very important man. He had a massive influence on shaping the education policies of the Blair government in the UK, and in driving policy 'delivery' more generally. He moved on to global consultancy roles, applying similar approaches to different parts of the world. He was the architect of the changes to school education in Punjab, which the World Bank is now supporting. I have known Michael - well, perhaps 'known of' would be more truthful - for a long time, off and on since we were both young Parliamentary lobbyists, but in recent years I have had the impression he would prefer not to be seen acknowledging me.

Surprise, then, this evening as Ian and I move towards the lovely Pakistani buffet, and there is Michael, taking the initiative to greet us in a friendly fashion. I wonder whether it is Ian's track record which has helped to tip the balance that way, but a nice moment, before Michael re-joins his entourage.

Later, in my room, I do a bit more work on the list of travels I had started transcribing from my diary. I ponder what to call the file. 'List of trips' is too boring. In the end I name the file 'Steps' because each of these trips feels like a step on a single big journey.

In the morning, Ian and I go back to DSD to flesh out some of the content of the legislation we are to write. Michael is there conducting a session with a large group of headteachers. He urges us to come and sit in on part of it to see what he is doing. He is wearing a beautifully tailored outfit of South Asian style. His session is about improving levels of school attendance, using performance data and target-setting in a spirit of friendly competition. In England, with its mature school system, many teachers and headteachers had hated this kind of data-driven competitiveness, but here it is a different story. Michael's policies had got the IT infrastructures in place to enable this kind of school management - in itself a miracle in the terrain of Punjab - and it is having a good effect. Such is Michael's global stature that for me to be seen as well regarded by him is enhancing my status with DSD.

Ian is well organised. In the car, he produces sanitiser and applies it to his hands, then reaches across offering to do mine. Instinctively I flinch away like a child. I don't explain that I have developed the habit of opening toilet doors with my feet when no-one is looking. Today's lack of water for washing has been an exception. Ian has been to India, which set certain expectations. He picked up quickly, as a pleasant surprise, the cleanliness, punctuality and general orderliness of Pakistan.

We call into the Programme Monitoring and Implementation Unit (PMIU) for a catch-up meeting with Dr Farah, and finish the day at the company's office with a project review meeting conducted by Roger, the most senior manager I have met so far in relation to this project.

These meetings, and a flurry of emails going this way and that, are partly the reaction to DSD's newly announced stance on its preferred way forward. Where does that leave all those great thick plans with their timelines and 'deliverables' and triggers for releasing funding? Umbreen, a senior official in the World Bank, says she wants a teleconference on Friday and a summit meeting early next week. Good! It feels as if something real is starting to happen.

The Avari Hotel has quite a few restaurants, although on this visit we are sticking to the main one. There is also a lounge menu of light snacks, which is a handy source of refreshment when working late. The main restaurant has a substantial walk-though buffet, always offering a predominantly Pakistani range of dishes, which are reassuringly different every day. The desserts section always includes an array of very decorative, fancily worked creamy confections that someone has taken a lot of trouble over. I never touch any of them; most days, nor does anyone else. I used to wonder about the condition of the milk and cream used, but someone told me it was all made from powdered products.

There are regular theme nights. The catering staff like showing off their versatility, although in reality they also show its limitations. Tonight is Caribbean Night, and as well as a banner saying so, there are flags on the tables to create the atmosphere. In the buffet, perhaps three dishes out of the many have distinctly Caribbean names, ingredients and appearance, although something about the textures and flavours remains Pakistani. Which doesn't matter at all, because I like Pakistani food, and pigging out on it is half the point of coming here.

On Thursday, Shahid, one of the guys from DSD, kindly takes us to visit a couple of schools. We go in his car, which being old doesn't have air conditioning, so from the outset we are exposed to hot, heavy humidity. Ian is suffering a bit from the side effects of the malaria tablets he is taking. I don't bother with them, and here the main threat is dengue, for which there is no medical protection. Warning signs are everywhere; they have enlarged pictures of mosquitoes with vicious expressions. Apart from covering up and avoiding stagnant water, the main precaution is window and door meshes. I don't like daubing on insect repellent, and in these weather conditions, it would not stay on for more than a few minutes.

The schools we see are both government-run secondary schools; both obviously picked as the good ones to show off to us. Against the standards of schools world-wide, they are certainly not bad, but against the standards of modern Western professional practice, they are in a time warp of between 30 and 40 years. This is how reasonable state schools in England might have conducted themselves in the 1960s.

One of the headteachers, who has won various accolades, proudly describes aspects of her work, but it is clear that she sees her work as finished if there is a teacher in every classroom. Despite my gentle probing, she does not see it as part of her job to lead the quality of teaching and learning. The other headteacher describes how she decides which children can come to her school by interviewing the children and their parents. It is not officially a selective school, but no-one sees anything odd in how this happens without criteria or systems to ensure fairness.

Among the new policies being implemented to improve schools is the provision of certain new textbooks and materials. So that this can happen, a drastic decision was taken recently that science must be taught in English. Many science teachers are not very fluent in English themselves. Ian and I watch a science lesson in which students are taking turns at reading out loud from the new materials. They decode the words with a bit of a struggle, but that is the main thing going on: an English lesson. I doubt they are learning much science.

My glasses steam up the moment I step outside an air-conditioned environment, which is frequently. In one of the schools, we are sitting talking with some staff, and someone proudly produces a tray of homemade snacks. Caution battles with greed, or to be accurate, my need to eat regularly to avoid getting headaches. Greed wins. There are cakes and some spicy, oily nuggets of something, which are very welcome.

The humidity has drenched my clothes. Today I have been wearing a blazer with maroon, navy and dark green stripes. When I take it off in the hotel, I see that the colours have run, and have made my shirt more interesting than it was.

In free times, Ian and I sometimes sit and work on our laptops in a lounge area near our rooms. I knew a fair bit about him before. On this trip I get to know more. He shares things I wouldn't have guessed about his early career, the path taken towards the notably senior positions he occupied. He has an interesting old house, in a quiet rural area I used to know. He is personally very disciplined, with the neat and tidy habits I would normally associate with ex-military people. His extensive work travel has included assignments in Russia, going to places frequented by armed gangsters. He is always supportive in how he contributes his expertise: an easy colleague to work with.

On Friday morning we are at the company's office for the teleconference with Umbreen at the World Bank. It is productive; we make arrangements for Monday's significant meeting. This is Ian's last day here. He will be replaced by my colleague Carol. It is my way of drawing in a range of different skills within a tight budget. After a bought-in lunch at the office, we go with Rosemary to DSD. Nadeem wants to 'say goodbye to Ian', but I would be surprised if he would make time just for that, so this will be interesting.

Nadeem is charming and very reasonable. He has obviously been got at by Umbreen and is agreeing to participate in Monday's meeting. The conversation is constructive and interesting. It makes a nice way to end Ian's visit because he has been a bit shocked by the state of affairs.

Ian's flight is in the middle of the night. We eat early so that he can get some rest. I come down when it is time for him to check out in case anything needs to be paid for, and to take possession of the phone, which he needs until the last minute to communicate with the driver. Not until I am back in London do I get to hear about Ian's dreadfully delayed journey. A Pakistan International Airlines jet crashed on the runway (PIA has a poor safety record) blocking all progress for many hours. Ian, already feeling poorly, had been crushed for ages amongst a dense crowd in the terminal, with only very basic dodgy refreshment.

My Saturday, in contrast to Ian's, passes in quiet, gently-paced deskwork in the hotel. I have a sore throat which I hope won't impair my authoritative speaking voice. I also have a runny stomach, and take three Imodium Instants (half my supply, but I have other things) because I am worried about getting through a long wait at the airport. I know that only those actually travelling are allowed inside the terminal. I am determined to meet Carol, whose flight is due at 1.50 am on Sunday, although everyone tells me it is unnecessary. The driver comes for me at 12.45 am. This particular driver is the best at protection: he is a proper ex-military bodyguard, but his English is limited. It is a strange new experience for me to be going to an airport here to meet an arrival.

We get there at 1.10 am, park and walk to the arrivals board, which is outside the building. It says Carol's flight will be about ten minutes late, so we go back and sit in the car, for what turns out to be an extended wait. That's not an issue for the driver. Periods of patient, watchful waiting are a normal part of a bodyguard's work. He stands outside most of the time. Among other things, he has been a long-range rifle sharpshooter: he can read the arrivals board from here, whereas for me the board is just a fuzzy blob of light.

The waiting period is less ordinary for me. For a start, I am aware of my dependent status. I am at the mercy of a man I can barely communicate with. What if he has arranged with some friends to kidnap me? What if he wanders off and doesn't come back? Base thoughts. I've been here enough to know that despite the range of problems this country has, the rock-solid reliability of its current and former military personnel is as much a national given as love of cricket.

I have brought nothing to do. Lamely I get out my old-fashioned, very primitive mobile phone and delete unwanted texts as a way of passing the time. The driver is concerned for my comfort, so he runs the engine periodically to make the air conditioning operate. But steaminess is also a big problem, so he opens the window a bit, which lets in insects. Without thinking, I squash one on my white jacket, making a messy cochineal stain several inches long.

The driver says the flight is announced as having landed. At 2.00 am we go and join the waiting throng. It is the only flight, even so, the formalities take a while, and Carol comes out at 2.45 am. She is surprised and pleased to see me, and comes forward clearly intending to kiss me, which I would enjoy. That is how we greet: not in the office, of course, but in circumstances like this. Regrettably, however, I don't want to risk offending the local cultural norms, so I hold up my hand in a stop sign, saying simply, 'Islam'.

Carol is as tall as me, slim, experienced, self-assured, a versatile and unflappable professional. She is also extremely easy to get along with. Six months ago, we spent a week working together in Delhi. It was like working with a family member or good friend - I could totally be myself, which takes a lot of stress out of these assignments. Back at the hotel, they put her in the room, which was Ian's, which is handily across the corridor from mine. I had wondered if they would put her in the ladies' wing.

I go to bed at 3.30 am, wake up (well, sort of) at 7.00 am, have a leisurely bath, and breakfast at 9.00 am. At 9.40 am I am sitting in the lounge area on the second floor, just along from my room, while the housekeeping guy finishes what he is doing. The staff are very pleasant and smiley and talk in a friendly way. I spend the rest of Sunday finishing the proposed legislation I have been drafting. Rosemary comes to eat with us at 7.00 pm to meet and brief Carol, especially regarding Monday's summit meeting. Carol is joining the stage at a point of high drama.

Monday's activity turns out to be a memorable highpoint in an otherwise plodding assignment. It's nice to get to do the sort of work I am paid to do. All the parties are here in the same room: the Schools Education Department, DSD and PMIU; the World Bank, the company, and of course our university. They are all behaving themselves. Who will preside? It will need to be either Umbreen from the World Bank or me. She gives me the nod. I say I will 'facilitate', much less threatening and presumptuous than 'chair'.

First I take the meeting through a memorandum of understanding I have written, setting out how the parties will work together on this project. That includes the proposed membership and functions of a steering committee. No-one disagrees, well not outwardly in front of the others. Today's meeting is, in effect, the first meeting of the steering committee. It is also the last, but that is another story. Then I talk them through other documents I have written: key clauses of a draft Bill to establish the new autonomous body, and key content for a prospectus describing its work. Everyone is happy, by which I mean that everyone is happy we have got to the end of the meeting. The day is steamy, and frequent power cuts mean there is often no air conditioning. In the car afterwards, Rosemary gets very cross about a little gnat and makes the driver stop and chase it out. There are probably a few more we haven't noticed.

Tuesday starts early. At 7.00 am, Carol and I meet to refine the plans for a workshop she is running tomorrow. Then at 8.00 am, Umbreen from the World Bank, and Mushtag from the Schools Education Department, come to have breakfast with us, so I must eat nicely, more like a polite gentleman, less like a greedy pig. The main thing they want to chew over is yesterday's meeting and how to consolidate a grip on the fragile beachhead that appears to have been established. Then we go to DSD for more detailed discussions, but the engagement I am looking forward to most is what I am doing at lunchtime.

Some while back, I met Uzma in London. She came to my office, and we chatted. Uzma is Director of Studies at a large and very prestigious chain of independent schools in Pakistan. When we met, she had recently completed a PhD (at another university) on aspects of school leadership and development very close to my own interests. She wanted to explore whether and how my organisation might work with hers to help her to implement some of that thinking. She has an office in Lahore; when she knew I was coming on other business, she suggested I drop in. I like doing that: dropping in when I am in a faraway city on other business. It makes me feel a bit of a globetrotter.

When I first explain this assignation to Rosemary, she struggles with it a bit. The company, with its blood-sucking, pound-of-flesh approach to management, naturally assumes it has bought me body and soul for the entire time of my stay. No, I explain patiently, it has bought a certain number of consultancy days each of a set number of hours (which I greatly exceed), and what I do outside that time is up to me. I do, however, need a car and driver, so I have to be very nice about it all.

I arrive at the headquarters building where Uzma works. I am met, she comes straightaway, all smiles and welcome, and leads me to her office. Now, a couple of things I need to explain to set the scene. My office in London is the average size someone at my sort of level would expect, in Bloomsbury, where floor space is at a premium. It has practical grade furniture, all covered with work clutter. I don't have servants to bring refreshments. When Uzma visited, she was in the dress and persona of an academic researcher. Here I am now, well looked after in a palatial, immaculate stylish ambience. Uzma is in her true persona as a very senior executive. Slightly embarrassed, I comment on the contrast. She laughs it aside, saying she knows what universities are like.

The second thing, which I didn't explain earlier in case you think I have a warped sense of priorities, is that as well as being clever and successful professionally, Uzma is incredibly beautiful. I mean seriously, out of this world beautiful, like a Bollywood actress only more so, with fine facial bone structure and big glittery eyes with long lashes. All that comes with a sweet disposition, soft gentle voice and lovely manner; she talks and listens attentively and respectfully, drinking in the conversation. As we sit two feet apart and I give her my keen attention, my mind is fully concentrated on research, and theories, and business models – honestly, of course it is. All the same, I feel wonderful.

Wednesday is Carol's workshop. She is really good at this sort of thing, and very adaptable to circumstances, which is useful. It is a wet day, with short stair-rod downpours. We have been allocated the conference room at DSD, which is not the best shape for small group interactive tasks. We have been warned the generator is not working, so given the frequency of power cuts, the company has kindly printed off the presentation. In the event, the projector and lights do work, but there is no air conditioning, so with 25 people in the room, the air is getting a bit unpleasant. Carol sets group discussion tasks with reporting back, which people engage in willingly. Speaking just for myself, I can't understand what anyone is saying, because of thick accents and racketing fans. People are happy; the mood is positive.

Next we have to go to the company's office, getting caught in another downpour as we arrive, for a 'contract compliance monitoring meeting'. This, predictably, is a long, unpleasant fencing match, reviewing the project 'deliverables', almost all of which were either ill-conceived at the outset by people without specialist knowledge, or have been rendered irrelevant or unachievable by changing circumstances. We soldier on and agree the next set of outcomes and timescales, all within the company's ethos of demand a lot, offer minimal support, pay the least they can get away with.

Carol and I stagger into the foyer lounge at the Avari Hotel. We are both very tired. We have discovered a useful light snack (lunch at the company's office was one biscuit each). It is a chicken-filled croissant with a small heap of coleslaw, served in the lounge, with plenty of tea. We are both determined not to talk about work. So we discuss a nearby lampshade, which is nicely crafted, of a pleasant design, with several interesting features. Then, er…well, we discuss the croissant. We move on to that euphemistically named task, 'work in own rooms', until it is time to go out again.

Umbreen comes with a young male colleague to take us out to dinner, which is very kind. She brings us to Salt'n Pepper Village. We go in, take our table, things start to happen, and only now do I realise I have been here before. It was during a power cut, which had given the place an exciting, dramatic atmosphere. Now, properly lit, it is quiet and plain by comparison, but much easier to see the food on offer. There is an extensive buffet including excellent charcoal-grilled kebabs, and bubbling cauldrons of this and that. I am happy to take my time here.

The desserts are interesting in their variety and ingredients. One of them is made out of kale.

Conversation flows pleasantly. The young man shoots partridges. I don't know how this topic has come up. As it happens, I enjoy playing with guns, although never involving living targets, but it isn't something I would raise in a mixed dinner party. He attacks them with a .22 rifle which must require very good marksmanship.

Thursday morning, and I oversleep badly. My deafness is getting worse: of course I don't wear hearing aids when sleeping. I had set two alarms for 5.30 am as usual; they must have rung and rung. Carol knocks on the door, I get out of bed and open it, and find I have five minutes to get ready for breakfast at 7.00 am. Today we have a series of wrap-up meetings, then we finish with work for now.

Carol and I will set off for the airport at 12.45 am. We have an early dinner, then walk around the hotel gardens. It is dark, but there is some lighting. I like seeing the numerous cats which live in the hotel grounds. The kitchen staff are kind to them. Some of them like to roost in trees as if they were birds. There are real birds: a big aviary of cockatiels. The strangest thing – I have never seen this before – is how they sleep. Clearly, they are asleep, clinging to various kinds of perches, oblivious to movement, not reacting to anything, frozen, motionless in odd postures, but their eyes are wide open, staring vacantly. It is weird, a bit ghostly, seeing them at close quarters like that.

After that pleasant, restful stroll, we wander into the hotel shop. We are the only customers. Carol wants to buy some fabric item as a gift. To keep her company I give in to temptation and buy a rug of nice quality, with some silk in its composition. Getting it into my suitcase is a tremendous challenge and requires me to throw away some things I can do without.

In odd moments of relaxation over the last two weeks, I have been adding brief notes to my list of trips, so that the document has grown to quite a number of pages. I write a final email home, with the latest bits of news and my flight times. After I have sent it, I have an idea. I copy and paste the email into the section of notes headed 'Step 36: Lahore'. It looks quite useful there as a memory aid. I copy in a few more of the similar emails I have sent recently. In the first few years of working internationally, I did not carry the equipment for sending emails. Then, when I did start to do so, a lot of that material got deleted later in periodic purges of my mailbox. A pity. I browse through 'sent' to see what I can find, what still exists. An hour has passed, and I have assembled 16,000 words of messy patchwork quilt. Raw material that is definitely not a basis for academic or professional writing. But definitely has the potential to be something.

This, Gentle Reader, is my birth as a travel writer. I am so glad that it is taking place here in the evocative ambience of the Avari Hotel Lahore. An apt starting point for another kind of journey.

Chapter Two

Karachi: Taking Time Out

I'll tell you a bit more before we set off for Karachi. First, migraine. Just a part of me, goes with the territory, that's the kind of person I am. The bad times were my teenage years, then in my mid-twenties. When I was at school, an aura would come on during a lesson. First, I couldn't decode words, or say them properly, or hold a pen or pencil, then vision would go entirely, then my speech would fail and the headache become intense and often not clear properly until the next morning. Some of the teachers hadn't got a clue. I couldn't explain why I couldn't function, was physically incapable of answering the question, 'What is the matter with you, you stupid boy?' So they would come and beat me about the head and shout abuse. One of the reasons I became an educationist. As I have grown older, headaches are not nearly so much of a problem, provided that I eat regularly and avoid migraine trigger foods, but auras continue to be a nuisance.

Another thing is that my wife Mary and I are, right now, in the middle (well at least I hope we have got that far) of a complicated house move. We are heading north, from Bromley, just to the south of London, to Barnard Castle in County Durham. The house we are trying to buy there, called Spring Grove, was previously split up, and we are buying our new home in two parts: a town house, and an adjoining ground floor flat. Fortunately both are for sale at the same time. To afford that, we have to sell two properties: the home we have lived in for a very long time, and an investment property. So two sales and two purchases have to slot into place, otherwise we are in a bit of a mess. That feels like quite a project, which includes a couple of gambles.

We like taking short breaks at Helmsley in the North York Moors. We started the habit in 1980, and that is where we are now, for a few days, a week before I set off back to Pakistan. We are staying at the Feversham Arms Hotel, as we did in 1980, but in those days it was the cheaper option, whereas now it has developed into a boutique hotel of taste, quality, pampering and indulgence.

We also like the carved oak furniture produced by Robert 'Mouseman' Thompson, so-called because each piece incorporates a mouse carved into its design. The company, named after its founder, is long-established and reputable because of the long period of traditional seasoning to which the oak is subjected, and the standard of craftsmanship. Many churches feature 'Mouseman' woodwork. Not surprisingly, it is hideously expensive. Our previous purchases had been at the scale of a wooden bowl, a cheeseboard, a three-legged milking stool, and, at the height of extravagance, a small octagonal table. When we viewed Spring Grove, I decided that the dining room's pleasantly oblong shape deserved to be filled with a 'Mouseman' refectory table. Our current oval dining table would go better in the library. The context of big spending for a major house move provides a 'now or never' excuse to acquire one of these modern antiques. The workshop and showroom are at Kilburn, quite near to Helmsley, so we go there, 'just to look'.

Looking is very nice. Looking, stroking, smelling – as sensual as a spa treatment, as aspirational as a Rolls Royce showroom. They tell us that everything is made to order, that what we want will take at least six months. So this is the first gamble. We can't yet be sure that we will get Spring Grove. If we don't, we will have nowhere to put these purchases. We take the gamble and come out into the cool moorland air having ordered a refectory table, a carver chair, six dining chairs and a Welsh dresser. I feel like a king.

I dine pretty well normally, but this evening feels celebratory. At the end of the meal, I ask, 'What is your best brandy?' The waiter, with some hesitation, almost apologetically, says, 'Well, our *very* best brandy costs £140 a shot.' 'Yes, we'll try that one, please', I say. There is method in this madness. I find with brandies that quality and price do not progress like a smooth upward curve on a graph. Above the level of everyday brandies, there seems to be a massive territory within which quadrupling of price may not necessarily produce any improvement in drinking experience, however hard I try to convince myself that it must be good because it cost a lot. One has to make a stratospheric leap to be sure of getting something memorable.

This has caused a little stir as if they don't sell it often. The sommelier arrives with a bottle moulded to look like an ice sculpture. He explains it is a top-end Richard Hennessy, incorporating very old eaux-de-vies. With laudable economy, we share the one shot. First, there is a strong cloud of aromatic vapour coming out of the glass, tingling and nose-clearing in its intensity. A sip, and then, pouf! A mouth-filling explosion of smooth heat, penetrating every pore and passage. I can almost taste it in my ears. This is what I was hoping for. Life as it should be. Money well spent.

I start my journey to Karachi on Sunday 30 September 2012, setting off from home in the morning. With hand luggage only, because I will be there for just a few days. Quickly getting reminded, surprised and disappointed all over again, at how poor travelling is on a Sunday. A longer wait for the bus, fewer trains into London. Then the tube trains are crowded, and the Circle and District lines are shut for engineering works. So I take the Victoria line to Green Park and change to the Piccadilly line for the long haul to Heathrow Terminal 3.

Through force of habit I go to check in, even though I don't really need to, but I like the comfort of knowing everything is in order. Security is a real scrum, packed with people partially undressing. I am told to go into the body scanning machine. I do hope they find the images attractive. Then at last into departures. It is such a relief to get there that it always feels like arriving, to begin with. The actual process of departing is something to start thinking about a bit later on. So, what shall I do now?

Lunch, of course. I make myself comfortable in the English restaurant called Rhubarb, and enjoy fish and chips, with Fentiman's ginger beer, a pot of Lapsang Souchong, and a phone call home. After, there is still plenty of time before my flight which leaves at 2.15 pm. I wander among upmarket shopping facilities. My means of travelling this morning did not involve spending on taxis or on the Heathrow Express. So really, I have been quite economical. These thoughts happen while I am standing by a posh seafood and champagne bar. A small portion of caviar later, I wander into Whisky Galore just to check something out. Yes, there it is (the shop isn't as narrowly specialised as its name implies), well back in its exclusive depths. The kind of Hennessy bottle I had last seen at the Feversham Arms, costing £1850. No wonder the hotel needs to price it as it does. Hmmm… I will have one of those in my sideboard one day. That day still hasn't come. The problem would be making it last.

I board the plane and find that I am travelling on one of the very large double-decker A380-800 Airbuses, new and nice with lots of imitation wood-effect plastic. I get comfortably settled in, and then a migraine aura starts during the safety presentation. This is the third in three days, which is unusual. On Friday afternoon, the actual trigger had been looking at the computer screen just after sending off my 'deliverables' for the Punjab project, so I think the underlying cause was the relief of having finished that tedious task.

On Saturday morning, yesterday, it was the opposite. I was on my way, for the very first time, to a meeting of a rifle club connected to my university, which uses a range hidden underground, deliberately hard to find, near to Blackfriars Station. That was pure anxiety: new activity, new location, new people to have to relate to. The same had happened some years previously when I had arrived at a shooting ground for my first proper shotgun lesson. I found it (eventually), parked the car, switched the engine off, and promptly lost it as my vision turned to a jazzy fuzz. Today, it's not so simple to attribute cause: probably a bit of everything.

Now, about this trip. This is my 'other' project in Pakistan. You remember, the one I said feels less like hard work, more like a holiday with friends. In 2010 we were approached by a small group of people based in Karachi, who wanted to make it possible for us to provide training courses and other kinds of development for teachers and school leaders in Pakistan. The leader of this initiative, a lively, affable guy called Taymur, became my kind host for each trip I made. The group set up a charity to give the initiative an identity. They called it Trust for the Advancement of Knowledge and Education (TAKE) and gathered in some philanthropic support to bring down the cost of my organisation's involvement. Which would be non-profit-making, but still expensive by local standards.

They got me there for a wonderfully educative and enjoyable familiarisation visit, then some months later, with colleagues, I ran courses in Karachi and Lahore. We needed to move away from the 'visiting expert' format, which just didn't feel right in this post-colonial age. So on my next visit, I tried a more interactive workshop, and out of that grew the idea of holding locally owned conferences with visiting speakers. Taymur came up with the name 'TAKE Time Out'; they would be held twice a year. The first took place earlier this year. Led by my colleague Eleanore, it was a triumph. She got the participants involved and energised, and organised a good number of them to work on projects in their own schools, to report back on in a year's time.

Today I am heading to the second of these conferences. This time the main inputs will be made by my colleague Hilary. I have worked with her previously in Delhi and Lucknow. She travels separately. I will run a seminar on instructional leadership, but apart from that, I don't really have much to do beyond showing general support. This is the kind of assignment I like best: a working holiday.

The flight is supposed to land in Dubai 15 minutes after midnight, but there is traffic congestion so we must sail around for a bit, at a speed just sufficient to stay airborne. In a smaller plane I sometimes find that motion queasy-making, but this one is big enough to retain a steady feel. The connecting flight is at 1.30 am. We drift about for half an hour waiting to land, which causes a rush and panic to make the connection. No time to send a text. Fortunately, there is a member of staff at the end of the exit tube, shouting 'Karachi!'

He gathers up the group who are going there, and rushes us on our way. One man says he wants to stop and buy chocolate, and is told, 'You buy chocolate or you catch your flight – no time for both!' The pace is brisk. We get to the now deserted gate and hurry through. I see a room full of people sitting and think they haven't gone on yet, but I can't see a door in the glass wall. That's a problem I have, a couple of times I have walked into glass by mistake. I stop and turn round to check my bearings. 'I think it's this way!' a man says, heading for a hole which is the tube leading straight on board. I find my seat and sit in it, expecting to feel motion almost immediately.

The first announcement says that we must wait for some more people coming off a connection, despite the rule that Emirates flights don't wait for latecomers. In the next announcement, the pilot explains that there is a slight technical problem, which the engineer will sort, but which will involve the need to 'depower', to switch everything off and on again. This will be interesting because during the safety briefings they say that if you have to leave the plane during a power cut, rows of lights on the floor will guide you. Now I have the chance to look out for them. There they are! Quite festive-looking rows of twinkles. They will cheer me up if I ever need to hurl myself into the sea.

The plane takes off. The only meal option is a very peppery chicken biryani, which is enjoyable, and if they can only manage one choice of dish, that one is sure to be pretty popular on this flight. The plane is only 30 minutes late arriving in Karachi, we land at 5.00 am. I pass through the formalities, not quickly or comfortably – that would be an exaggeration, but certainly a lot less tediously than sometimes. Having no suitcase to collect, I can walk straight out, where a hotel driver is waiting. He drives quickly, so I reach the Avari Towers Hotel at 6.00 am. Always a pleasant, reassuring, homecoming experience. This is my fifth visit, the fifth time the reception staff find papers marked, 'Gratis: guest of Mr Avari', and escort me to my room, taking their already faultless standards of courtesy and hospitality up to an even higher level, as if I was someone important. I make tea, then go to bed for a few hours.

Late morning, I am up and attending to emails, then go to the foyer to meet Taymur, who says that Colin is on his way. Meanwhile, a waiter passes me an oval dish, with a folded towel at one end, and a little glass of chilled cinnamon tea at the other, equipped with a cinnamon stick to stir it with. This part of the lounge is called the Cinnamon Bar, and there are cinnamon sticks aplenty as an aromatic element of the décor.

Colin is an elderly Englishman who has lived in Pakistan for most of his life, the long-serving Principal of Karachi Grammar School. He is at or near the point of transitioning from that to his own business, which involves buying small, struggling independent schools, developing them to a good standard, and selling some of them on. Colin is a friend to Taymur, and to our project, which he has supported loyally from the start. His wife was Pakistani, she died, he home educated their son. A decent guy with vast local knowledge.

Colin arrives, Taymur says he is keen to go to the Japanese restaurant on the top floor of the hotel, which I have not been to previously, and where we settle at a table by the window. Now here is a different view. Interestingly, Colin seems as taken with it as I am. On my four previous visits, I studied the views from my bedroom windows which faced at least two different directions, neither showing anything remarkable, so I never really got a handle on what I was looking at, where the hotel was in relation to other parts of the city. When I was driven to places, I tried to make sense of the routes but never succeeded.

To me, Karachi seems to be a sprawling, modern, pulsating place of commerce without obvious urban form. Modern in the sense that apart from a small seaport, there was not much to Karachi 200 years ago. Now it has a population of 20 million. It's easier to get the picture where there is a major historic town centre with concentric rings of growth around it. It's easier where a city is built on a mountainside or has other prominent physical features. The site Karachi was built on is not flat, but the coast is really the only natural landmark. The maps I have been able to find are of poor quality and not very informative. I mention that to Colin. He says he has better ones at school, he will give me one. That makes me feel better already. An ex-geography teacher without a map or bearings feels like a fish out of water.

It is a clear, sunny day. As usual, many red kites are circling around. Colin is studying some distinctive rooftops, checking out what he can see, getting his bearings from the clearly-labelled Marriott Hotel tower block, which is well away to the extreme right of our panorama. This is really useful. I encourage him to elaborate. Nearby, straight in front, is a large old building which looks a bit like a cathedral. Colin says it is Frere Hall. Originally intended as a town hall and library, it was built between 1863 and 1865, to a design chosen from among numerous suggestions. The successful architect was Henry Saint Clair Wilkins (no relation, so far as I am aware, but genealogy can be full of surprises). I don't know if he ever received formal training as an architect: he seems to have been a career army officer with the East India Company, rising to the rank of general. He served in a number of campaigns and became an aide-de-camp to Queen Victoria.

Alongside those military accomplishments, Wilkins became skilled in architectural and engineering works. He restored ancient water tanks in Aden, restored and adapted ancient buildings in Orissa, and won first prize in a competition with his design for a hospital in Bombay. At Poona, he designed a hospital, a college, a synagogue and a mausoleum. And so on – his designs seem to have been regarded as tasteful by the fashions of the day.

His winning design for Frere Hall made it of Venetian Gothic style, incorporating rows of pointed arches, ribbed vaults, flying buttresses and a tall octagonal tower. No wonder I thought it looked like a cathedral. It is constructed of different coloured local limestones and sandstones, arranged to give vibrant patterns of red, yellow, white and grey. The building is surrounded by lawned gardens. All in all, quite a statement for a town hall and library: nothing utilitarian or minimalist here.

Next, Colin draws my attention to a smaller old building, down to the left, nearer the hotel. This is Quaid-e-Azam House, for some years the private home of Muhammad Ali Jinnah, the founder of Pakistan. 'House' is slightly modest: palatial mansion would be a better description. It is an attractive two-storey building surrounded by mature gardens. It is now a museum. So these really important historical edifices were right on the doorstep, and I never knew they were there. One of the downsides of not being able to wander about outside on my own.

Menus arrive and orders are placed. I am happy to let them take charge. Taymur says he will just have a starter and no main course because he has a poorly stomach. He dismisses any question of what might have caused it. 'It could be anything', he says and draws his finger across the surface of the table. 'You could get it just by doing that!'

In addition to Taymur's quite substantial starter, the food brought to the table includes miso soup, tempura, sushi, teriyaki chicken and rice. There also seem to be several additional small bowls of fluids of different kinds. I am not totally confident that I can guess the purpose of each. Drink like tea? Dip other foods into it? Wash my fingers in it? Pour it over rice? Best to hold back cautiously, always willing to learn.

Over the meal we talk about arrangements for tomorrow, ideas for future TAKE events, and whether and how we might work with the government sector, including any possible link with my work in Punjab. We finish with lychees and ice cream, and a call comes through to say that Hilary has arrived from the airport. We go down to meet her, but of course, her main need is for some rest.

I also need some time in my room. I check emails. Mary has forwarded one about a lesson I have booked for Saturday at a shooting ground near to our second home, which is in Withernsea, on the Yorkshire coast. It is Mary's old family home, which she inherited. I need to study an article I have given as a set reading for my seminar tomorrow. I start reading it but am drowsy. I try the usual tricks: reading standing up, reading while drinking tea, reading while breathing deeply. Then give up and take a siesta, and get the job done when I wake up.

I go down to the foyer just before 7.00 pm. Colin comes through the entrance door and says that Taymur is waiting in the car. Reception phones Hilary's room – she has just been finishing an email. Taymur drives us to the commander's house where, amid pleasant wafts of incense, I enjoy a stiff gin and tonic, and bring him up to date with this and that. The commander is retired from the Pakistan Navy, but still very actively networked with everyone who matters. He is a prosperous businessman and is involved with philanthropy, politics and cricket. He is also Chair of Trustees both of Taymur's school, and of TAKE. He likes alcohol, and his house is always awash with it. That was a perverse culture shock when I first came here, having worked in Saudi Arabia and Yemen. I expected to remain dry in a dry country. I expect in any country not to drink when I am working. Strange that this should be the place where I learnt to relax a bit. We don't linger because we have a dinner date.

The commander's house is in Clifton. That I do know, and can find the general area on a map. It is an oblong peninsula between the Arabian Sea and Gizri Creek. It is a high-class residential neighbourhood. On my first visit, Taymur took me to his school, which is sited here among the tree-lined avenues of Old Clifton, near to Mohatta Palace. Mohatta Palace is a museum, built in 1927 (so in the days of pre-partition India) in Indo-Saracenic style for a Hindu businessman from Rajasthan as his summer residence.

Taymur drives us the short distance to Okra, which is located a few hundred yards north-east of Mohatta Palace in a busy sidestreet of restaurants in Zamzana, at the western end of Clifton, a mile or so inland from the Arabian Sea. Staff take the car away to find somewhere to park it. This valet parking is very common here. It involves trust, it would bother me a bit. We are dining with Barbara, from the British Council, who arrived shortly before us. Okra is busy, booking essential, with an intimate feel. There is an upstairs, reached by a narrow winding staircase, but today we are downstairs next to the enormous grill, where the cooking process is open to view. Although the restaurant is quite small, there are roughly 90 staff. That includes car-parkers, but still a lot work in the kitchens, where virtually everything is prepared from scratch. The cuisine is Mediterranean and Middle Eastern. There is a wide range of freshly baked breads in European styles.

Barbara has recently been appointed as the Head of British Council for Baluchistan and Sindh, the two provinces which make up the southern third of Pakistan. This will be a three-year placement for her, following similar assignments in Tokyo, Caracas and Ethiopia. We chat easily and broadly across the educational topics of common interest.

The furniture and fittings are stylishly simple, mainly in blue-greys. The crudites on the table include okra, of course, as well as very pleasant crisp sticks of some kind of beetroot. I have ginger beer, vegetable broth, then 'black seared rare beef', which sounds interesting. Mercifully, the waiter asks, 'Do you actually want it rare, or would you prefer medium?' Grateful for the option, I choose the latter. It is excellent: neat little slices with crisp and flavoured outsides, moist and tender. That comes with some leaves, and cold cooked potato with mustard. Enjoyable, but my body is starting to remind me that I came off a flight at 5.00 am that morning, after having been travelling for 16 hours. The restaurant is filled with conversation, a level of background noise that makes my hearing aids ineffective.

On the drive back, at last I start to get some bearings. We are heading north. In the distance, to my left, so north-west, I spot the Marriott Hotel, with its name in giant red illuminated letters. After a while, we pass Frere Hall on the right. Then we take a right turn, and near to the corner we are turning round is the Sind Club. This exclusive gentlemen's club has retained the old spelling of Sind from the time of its founders. The official modern spelling of the name of the province is Sindh. The commander is a member of the Sind Club, and on my first visit to Karachi he threw a garden party in my honour, and bought in the Club's caterers. It was an impressive occasion. Then ahead on the right is Quaid e-Azam House, and on the left is the Avari Towers Hotel. It has at least two entrances, but coming in this way has helped me to understand the lie of the land. At last.

Hilary and I are dropped off and we make our way through the security doors. The guards obviously think we look harmless. Hilary wants to see where we will be working tomorrow, so I check with reception and they show us two very spacious interlinked rooms on the lobby level, which is ideal.

Tuesday, and I am up early because conference registration opens at 7.30 am. A reasonable crowd assembles, and a pleasant, friendly atmosphere builds. The first session is for the whole gathering. Then, during a break, the room divider is put in place, and at 11.00 am, I start a seminar in one of the spaces, with about 35 headteachers, while Hilary works with the rest of the attendees in the other space. A very good buffet lunch is enjoyed in the hotel's main eating area, then I continue with my group until 3.00 pm. During another break, the room divider is removed, and the conference continues in plenary session. After the formal business, everyone is marshalled into place for a group photograph. Then I relax in my room, sipping mint tea, until 7.30 pm when we set off to attend the commander's party.

The commander hosts a party every time I come to Pakistan to work on this project. He is a generous entertainer. I couldn't begin to estimate what each of these gatherings costs. He is always able to draw together a large crowd of interesting, useful people in relevant positions. It is the same today. His spacious house is heaving with groups engaged in lively conversation, and tables are set with delicious buffets. Everyone has a glass of something. This evening, I feel slightly unwell, and don't work the room or gorge the refreshments with quite my usual enthusiasm.

On Wednesday morning, I am definitely under the weather. I have a thick head-cold, my stomach is upset, and my arm and shoulder are very painful, which I assume is a long-term effect of a car accident I had nearly a year ago. I am glad I don't need to do anything. I sit with Colin and Taymur at a side table, watching Hilary entertaining the group. They seem to like it. She seems to have established a resonance.

I will be starting my journey home this evening. The conference continues tomorrow, but I am not needed, and at the time the arrangements were being made, I had booked myself in as a guest at a function in the House of Commons tomorrow evening. Later, I email Mary to say I shan't be attending that event: it would have been nice, but too much on top of travelling, and no-one will be bothered by my absence. I resolve to find a physiotherapist near to my office.

My week finishes with an appointment at the Chamberlain's Court in the City of London, on Friday, for a short private ceremony at which I am made a Freeman. This is not any kind of honour or distinction. It is called 'Freedom by Redemption' and helps an organisation I support to progress to the status of a livery company. On Friday night, I drive to Withernsea, ready for my shooting lesson on Saturday. The owner of the shooting ground, Paul, is a very skilled instructor. I don't know how he does it, whether some tiny nudges are involved, but under his tutelage, I hit targets I would miss on my own. Sometimes, when I shoot a flying bitumen disc into fragments, I wish some other issues could be resolved like that.

Chapter Three

Gandhinagar: Modi's Backyard

It's time to introduce you to Joyce, you'll meet her properly later on. My work has been a lonely business over the last few years. That may sound odd when I am part of a big organisation. But like others of its kind, its culture is quite competitive and individualistic. From the time I switched to specialise in international consultancy, I have had to be self-reliant. The administrative team control their side of things, but finding jobs to do, and doing them, is down to me. When colleagues come with me on a project, they are either freelancers, like Ian, or they are people with their own full-time jobs, like Carol, fitting in my project as a bit of a favour. If I am away working with a client for a week or so, I may have to keep dialogues going convincingly with other actual or potential clients, which can be a bit demanding without any back-up.

It was a pleasant surprise, and great relief, when a new post was created back in the summer for a senior professional person to support and deputise for me. Joyce was appointed, and it has been wonderful having her to talk everything through with. Her background, like mine, is professional rather than academic. We will work together comfortably. Of course she is itching to get started on some international work and to get a project she can lead. Next, I need to explain - don't worry, we'll be getting off to Gandhinagar soon - another welcome development back in the summer. I was asked to become involved in a large and significant project which has been running for a few years and has just one more year to go. There have been some problems, especially a difficult working relationship with the client. The project concerns research rather than consultancy; the team working on it includes several senior academics, a research assistant and an administrator. I was asked to join the team in a sort of managerial role, to help to guide the project to its conclusion as smoothly as possible.

The project involves a number of Indian states, and it concerns initiatives within those states to implement aspects of global 'good practice'. A large team of Indians in senior positions has been making study visits around the world to learn about 'good practice' in various aspects of education, and they have been leading and supporting local initiatives in each of the states involved.

One of the states is Gujarat. My first real work on this project (apart from internal meetings and a lot of background reading) is to be part of a three-day workshop which is taking place in Gujarat. The other members of the delegation will be Edward, who is the senior academic in overall leadership of the whole project, and Marie, who is an academic specialising in South Asian affairs. Edward and I set off from London at 9.25 pm on Saturday 21st of October. Marie is already in the region.

Finalising the dates for this workshop, from the options the client suggested and around our availabilities, has been part of an extended juggling act going on presently. The balls (knives? – it feels like that sometimes) represent various actual and potential work commitments and my planned house move. I am juggling away, then one or two balls vaporise, which comes as a disconcerting let-down.

There is an immensely exciting trip in the diary, offering the opportunity for Joyce and I to do a first assignment together in rural Bangladesh. Amazing stuff. We are due to fly to Dacca on 29 November. Before then, I ought to get back to Punjab to do the next bit of work on the teacher licensing and certification project. There is also a project running in Colombia, which I started just over a year ago. When I visited in the summer (just 'dropping in' on the Ministry, like I did on Uzma), they said they would be wanting me back in the autumn.

The Colombians tell us at short notice that they need a presence on the ground for a week and a half, covering the dates I have already committed to the Gujarat workshop. So Colombia becomes Joyce's initiation. The work involves evaluation, so there is merit in deploying a fresh pair of eyes. Can I fit in a trip to Punjab between Gujarat and Bangladesh? On Thursday, before parting for our current trips, Joyce reminds me I will have to help her with the report of her Colombian visit, which is needed in mid-November.

That means I don't have time to fit in Punjab. I arrange for Ian to go with a brilliant young academic in the department here, who can write books and articles as easily and quickly as I write shopping lists. His name is Chris B. I don't include surnames in this book, but another Chris appears later on. I don't want to give either of them a different name, because I am synesthesic, and like the look of the word 'Chris'. Pink 'c', beige 'h', dark green 'r', opalescent 'i' and yellow 's'. There's a nugget of personal information for you! After making these arrangements, the lovely Bangladesh assignment gets cancelled at the last minute, so I go from overstretched to underemployed. A vaporising ball.

There are also uncertainties on the home front. On Tuesday of this week, we are due to exchange contracts for the sale of our home, but instead, our buyer pulls out. Another ball vaporises. I ask the vendor of Spring Grove to hang on for us. We are back at square one, inviting fresh viewings. Our packing is well advanced, some of our rooms are stacked with removal boxes. Some of the things in them are things we need - we packed them because we hadn't expected still to be here.

Meanwhile, the sale of our investment property is proceeding smoothly: completion happens the day I get back from Gujarat. So here is the other big gamble we have to consider. Do we proceed with buying the lease of the ground floor flat at Spring Grove, using the proceeds of the sale of the investment property, in the hope that the rest of the transaction will happen? If it doesn't, the leasehold of the flat is of little practical use: there is a limit to how many residences a busy couple can spread themselves across. It would not be possible to sell it on, except at a very heavy loss. But if we delay, the flat could be withdrawn from the market or sold to someone else, so we wouldn't be able to reunite the building for our use. We have to take the gamble and proceed.

I host some fresh viewings of our home, including two on Saturday before I set off for Heathrow to meet Edward. I have known Edward for about ten years. I was a consultant on a team he was leading at a previous university. His brother is a director of education in local government, as I used to be, so there is a point of common interest. He is about the same age as me, thorough and careful in his approach, and reads a lot: it is rare to see him without a book in his hand to dip into in any free moment. He has written over 40 books of his own, all based on serious research. That is reflected in his lecturing style, which is usually mainly a formal exposition of quite dense material.

We are flying to Mumbai, still identified as 'Bombay' in international airport abbreviated code letters. Amongst his hand luggage, Edward carries a classy leather accessory which holds his passport and travel documents. Too bulky for me to want one, but it makes a statement. He also carries a serious-looking book to read, to which he gives his attention for most of the flight. I am equipped with a more diverting book.

An acquaintance e-mailed recommending Peter Carey's novel *The Chemistry of Tears*, saying 'it is about your new next-door neighbour'. I bought it in the branch of Waterstones near my office that, having used it for decades, I shall always think of by its former name of Dillons. I am very happy to read Peter Carey. I have enjoyed several of his novels for their original subject matter, detailed research, visualisation and convincing writing. You believe you are reading history; you believe you are standing in his setting.

By 'our next-door neighbour', I assume our friend is referring to the Bowes Museum, which is very near to Spring Grove. In the shop, I skim through the book to see what she means. I see that the novel is about the automaton swan that is one of Bowes's most popular exhibits. It does not mention the Bowes Museum. The story has two settings of time and place: a modern-day museum in London where the automaton is being restored, and historic settings in Germany where it is being made. I set off to Gujarat, taking Peter Carey with me, reading it from cover to cover during this assignment. The story contains much sadness. The design, construction and restoration of the automaton are researched and presented in meticulous detail. It is hard to remember that this is a work of fiction, and yet it is. The actual origins of the swan, in Paris, are known. This one exhibit seems to have inspired Carey's creativity and imagination: as usual, with poignancy. The story strengthens my affection for the Bowes Museum and pleasure in the prospect of living next door. It also heightens the discomfort of uncertainty about the sale of our house.

Just over nine hours, and just under 4500 miles, since leaving Heathrow, we land at Chhatrapati Shivaji International Airport in Mumbai. Having travelled east across time zones, it is still only 11.00 am here, which makes the night flight seem even more tiring. Our domestic flight leaves at 1.55 pm. We make our leisurely progress through the formalities. The official dealing with us at immigration is a memorable character. He has developed languid insouciance to an artform, sprawled back in a chair, looking down his nose at our papers. I can't help noticing, with slight amusement, the contrast to the snap and polish of Pakistani officials, who stamp documents with a parade-ground flourish. Edward reacts differently. When the official has finished with Edward's passport, he flicks it towards him with a minimal but effective motion of his middle finger. Might that have been a reaction to the fancy leather case? Neither of us get a smile, or word of welcome, just a cold, superior stare. Edward is offended. For a moment, it looks as if he might make an issue of it, but fortunately, he waits until we are on our own. 'Did you see how he treated us, with total disdain?'

Our flight to Ahmedabad takes just over one hour. We are met and taken by car about 15 miles north to Gandhinagar, which is now (since 1970) the capital of the state of Gujarat. It is a modern city, named after Gandhi, who was born in Gujarat, and designed by Indian planners and architects. Building started in 1966. Ahmedabad had been the previous state capital, supposedly founded by Sultan Ahmed Shah in the fifteenth century. We are driven to where we are lodging, at the Cambay Spa and Golf Resort, which is a modern construction of red brick, set in a rectangle of pleasant grounds, within the grid pattern of a high-tech industrial estate. As always, it's nice to arrive, especially because the standard of accommodation is very good.

Gujarat is the westernmost state of India, on the Arabian Sea. Its next-door neighbour to the west is the Pakistani province of Sindh. Gujarat is roughly a couple of hundred miles in each dimension, so it is a bit larger than Wales, a bit smaller than Scotland. Unlike either of those places, the climate in Gujarat is very dry all year round except for the eastern areas which catch the monsoon. Summers are hot. Among Gujarat's ancient wonders are the stepwells created deep underground between the eleventh and fifteenth centuries, some of them palatial in scale, and beautifully decorated.

The western half of the state includes large areas of coastal desert and marshland which are important for wildlife. The eastern half is industrial, forming part of the crescent-shaped corridor of development between Delhi and Mumbai. The edge of a tectonic plate runs through Gujarat towards its western border, and there was a major earthquake in 2001.

I have a strong sense that our visit here has two agendas. The first is the overt and official business of running a workshop. Alongside that, I feel that I have come to take part in a summit meeting because of the long-standing tensions and disagreements between our team and the client. I hope that we will be able to achieve some thaw, rapprochement, breakthrough even – or at least to rub along well enough for the project to proceed with a workable level of cooperation.

We have a sizeable hall as our teaching space. The equipment and facilities are fine. I greet Marie, who I know from previous meetings; this will be the first time I have seen her in action. There are about 40 workshop participants, in addition to the client, represented by Anthony, who organises everything, and Renu, who is the overall boss, and a few of their support staff. Also in the room are some local dignitaries from the State of Gujarat. The workshop participants are mainly teams from the participating states, some of whom work at state level and some at district level. In addition, there are representatives of national organisations which are involved with the project. Not having met any of them before, all I see right now is a roomful of talkative, confident, assertive people. Someone calls the room to order, and a Hindu prayer is sung, and tapers are lit. I am slightly surprised. I don't mind, of course – always happy to experience the local culture. But I've worked in India before, and on only one occasion encountered any compulsory religion at the start of a professional development event, and that was very overtly multi-faith, the overall boss on that occasion being a Baha'i. I know India has a secular constitution, and that given its location, Gujarat must, historically, have had significant Islamic influence, and that Jainism also has a presence here. So I wonder a bit.

Anthony is the first to speak, followed by the commissioner for higher education. During that talk, Gujarat's secretary for education arrives and creates a space for herself at the centre of the top table by making everyone else shuffle sideways to less important positions. Next, I am invited to say a few words about the workshop, for which I adopt the ambassadorial voice and gravitas I consider appropriate when formally representing my organisation. When I have finished doing that, there seems to be a pause, and these ceremonies have already delayed the schedule for the workshop by half an hour, so I modulate to my normal professional persona and start explaining how the workshop will operate. Anthony stops me. He is agitated, and he explains that the secretary will speak next. Oh dear, I've done it again, this is always happening, but I didn't have an order of service handy. The secretary's speech is forceful. It doesn't really have much content, certainly not of any noticeable relevance to this workshop or the project in general, but projects a clear message. That is, 'I, and the government of which I am an important part, are in charge around here. Of everything. Got that?'

In my naïve and stereotyping way, I associate India with a gentle, tolerant, philosophical spirituality, but I'm not getting that today. This is much more like working in Saudi Arabia, where power, pecking order and deference are prominent in any meeting involving officials. Interesting.

We get going. The workshop is about teacher training. This is one of the issues which has been raised by the states participating in the project. We will be helping the group to think through various aspects of the initial (pre-service) training of teachers, and their in-service training: that is, their ongoing professional development throughout their careers. The delegates have done some pre-workshop tasks, reviewing current practice in their states.

The main pattern of activity for the first two days is a series of lectures by Edward, interspersed with a series of group work sessions organised by Marie. These follow a format which she explains is called World Café. It involves structured discussions of prepared topics in small groups, the membership of which changes part-way through the session. This is new to me, it is interesting to see a fresh approach. It requires quite active facilitation. The participants engage well and seem to find it useful.

The tea breaks are taken in another room nearby, where there is a large urn of milky chai. I normally drink black tea, and I am suspicious of dairy products in hot countries. But hey! It's India, I'm thirsty, I need tea, so I end up drinking as many cups as I can of this sweet, creamy, pudding-flavoured mixture. The group spread themselves out onto the pleasant lawn during these breaks. Lunch and dinner are taken in the hotel's main eating area. The offering is broadly similar on every occasion: a vegetarian buffet, in which pulses feature prominently. Dried lentils and beans are an important source of nourishment in an arid region. I notice the absence of meat and also the absence of alcohol. Not that I want any, it is just that these absences are noteworthy in a four-star hotel in a country which is not officially 'dry'. Somehow alcohol comes up in conversation, and someone, I think probably Anthony, says, 'Well, a hotel of this grade would probably be able to get some in for a Western visitor, but they wouldn't like doing so.'

Gradually I pick up more about the local politics, especially from Marie. South Asian affairs are her area of expertise. The chief minister of Gujarat is Narendra Modi (who progressed in 2014 to become Prime Minister of India). Modi was born in Gujarat, and at the age of eight began a long association with a Hindu nationalist volunteer force called Rashtriya Swayamsevak Sangh (RSS). He became a full-time worker for them at the age of 21. He joined the Bharatiya Janata Party (BJP) with RSS encouragement and support and moved swiftly up its ranks. He started his tenure as chief minister of Gujarat in 2001, and we are here in October 2012, so he has had time to stamp his mark. Modi's intolerance towards religions other than Hinduism is his trademark. There were major anti-Muslim riots in Gujarat in 2002, and although no blame has been pinned on Modi personally, there is substantial and prolonged speculation that the riots were, at the least, passively condoned by the government. Modi's policies in Gujarat favoured economic, business and infrastructure development, in which fields some significant successes were achieved, although this was at the expense of social welfare which was given lower priority. It might be my imagination, but I sense that right-wing, intolerant attitudes have somehow permeated the fabric of the place.

Renu and Anthony have arranged a treat for us. They are taking us out to dinner. As usual in such situations, I have only the vaguest understanding of what is actually happening. Only that we will be getting a Rajasthani culinary and cultural experience. Sometimes it strikes me how trusting we have to be on these assignments: getting into a car driven by someone we don't know, being whisked off into the twilight to an address we don't know.

Research long after the event enables me to say that we are heading for an evening at Chokhi Dhani Rajasthani Village Fair and Dining. This organisation is a franchise offering a particular kind of visitor attraction. I never do get to know precisely where we are, certainly it isn't one of the locations featured on the organisation's website when I get to the stage of looking for it. Perhaps that particular franchised outlet had gone out of business by then. We enter a sort of theme park and amble about among the attractions. Rajasthan is the state to the north of Gujarat, and the exhibition is supposed to depict aspects of Rajasthani village life, crafts and culture. Which it does up to a point: the attractions are either in booths or in open sand-filled enclosures. There are some crafts going on, and some magic tricks being performed, juggling, other circus skills, and various activities in which children might like to participate. It's all a bit pseudo. It has about it something of the unconvincing amateurishness of sideshows at a parish garden party. Fortunately, it's getting dark, and we are led indoors. 'Indoors' gives a first impression of a lavish, richly decorated interior, in which female greeters wearing embroidered costumes in bright colours usher us along a corridor.

Clumping, echoey footsteps make me realise quickly that, in fact, this 'palace' is a wooden hut, with wall surfaces covered in ethnic designs. We come to an eating area, which is a large oblong hut with an open front. Around the three walled sides, there is an arc of monks' prayer stools with a kneeler in front of each. No, I have got that wrong. Some diners have already arrived; they are sitting on the cushion, and the small item of furniture is a table which fits across their thighs.

It's a while since I have dined sitting on the floor. Five years since I had a delightful feast in The Village in Riyadh, which offers an authentic Arabian experience. My joints seem to have deteriorated a lot since then. I try, I genuinely try to battle indignity and discomfort, but after about three minutes I know I can't last much longer, and tell one of the staff I need a chair. He brings one, and I feel an awful old crock sitting on a throne among a floor-level group, but later feel relieved not to be trapped under one of the heavy lap tables.

It's a single sitting, communal dinner. The waiters wear supposedly traditional ethnic costumes. When all the places are full, things start to happen. Starters, for starters: various pakoras and other small snacks, prettily presented on a bit of banana leaf with a tangy dip. Main course begins with a swoosh of powder on the round metal plate. Is it ground almond, I wonder? No, I try a pinch and it is biscuit crumbs. Rich Tea, probably. Which I think is odd, but then remember the pile of breadcrumbs which lands on one's plate at Rules, followed after a decent interval by a quick-roasted grouse. Dishes arrive one after the other, creating a thali, which I assume represents the flavours of Rajasthan. Certainly a lot of lentils and other pulses are involved, and things containing yoghurt. Syrupy dumplings follow. Overall, not bad, it's different, and I like eating, but not that memorable either. I guess that in Rajasthan this food would probably be more workers canteen than fine dining. We get to our feet – much easier for me than for the rest of the party, and make our way to where the cars are waiting. I am aware of having eaten quite a lot. The return drive gives me no greater sense of location or direction than I had before.

The workshop continues. An expert from a national organisation in India concerned with teacher training gives a lecture on recent developments, bringing a fresh voice and welcome variety to our routine. By now, my stomach is upset. The toilet attached to this conference suite is outside, by which I mean the cubicle door opens directly onto the path and lawn. The light doesn't work, the door fitting is wonky, and the seat slides about, but despite those limitations, it becomes my regular place of comfort.

Renu, Anthony and their assistants usually sit with us at mealtimes. I feel that at a personal level we are interacting well. Edward remains reserved and cautious. His issue is that the way the project has played out over the last few years has differed in various significant respects, to the disadvantage of our organisation, from what the original contract said. That is certainly factually accurate, and it is in Edward's nature not to let it go but to keep on disputing the matter, making interactions argumentative. I am coming fresh to the situation. I like Renu as a person, and am inclined to take a pragmatic view. Some work is going on, which seems to be quite useful; we are getting paid for it, at least up to a point.

Dengue is still a problem, despite the wet season being over, and it has been rife wherever Renu lives. Her son is currently in hospital being treated for it. Over lunch, a mosquito comes to look at what we are eating. Someone shouts a warning. 'Oh I don't think they look like that', opines Edward, nonchalantly, showing that his erudition does not stretch to entomology. Meanwhile, Renu, who has good reason not to like them, launches herself across the table, clapping her hands, and finally achieves the kill while laying among the dishes.

Wednesday, the last day of the workshop: Edward and I will fly off this evening. After an early breakfast, we have a team meeting, after which Edward says to me, 'So now we need to check out of our rooms.' Without thinking, and deferring to his seniority, I go along with that, and spend the rest of the day regretting it. Why have we done this? Normally, whether at work or on holiday, I hang on to a hotel room until the last possible moment. Here, its attractions are its superior internet connection and its lovely bathroom.

Our teaching work ends early afternoon, with the usual reflection and feedback activities. Renu takes charge and leads a formal closing session, in which some of the participants are invited to speak. A couple of education officials from the government of Gujarat add their remarks.

After the participants have left, and we have had cups of tea, we have a formal meeting with Renu and Anthony – this had always been part of the schedule – to take stock of everything. I find it interesting and, overall, reasonably constructive and good-natured. The setup is complicated. The project is funded by the European Union, and the client is the Indian branch of an aid agency that operates globally. The work our organisation is doing is like a sub-contract, but between our client and the EU, there is a steering committee involving other influential Indian agencies, and which takes policy decisions that impact our work.

It becomes apparent that there have been some genuine misunderstandings by the client about what our share of the funding would cover and how universities work: a new one arises now. We are told the EU needs to see the contracts of employment of our team. Which is unusual, and it brings out Edward's pugnacity. 'They are confidential! It would be illegal for us to give them!' he ripostes. 'I need to see the law that says that,' Renu counters. So not totally a love-in yet.

There is dead time to fill, before we need to set off to the airport. Our flight is at 9.50 pm. Marie has headed off elsewhere in the region. Edward and I settle ourselves in a sort of lounge area not far from the reception desk. There is not much to it, just a few easy chairs and a glass-topped table filling an alcove. Actually I am not at all settled. This place and activity hold few attractions for me. If I had the use of my room, I could be making tea using my own teabags, using the bathroom as often as I feel inclined, and lolling on the bed, perhaps. Instead of which, I have to behave like a grown-up. What a bore!

Edward decides to do some work on his laptop. He is writing his next academic book and likes working to tight deadlines. But the glass-topped table isn't in the right place. It is against a wall, whereas he needs it in front of his settee. He gets up and starts to move it. Its timber frame is heavier than he expected, so he changes from a lifting to a dragging motion. It shudders protestingly across the rough flagstones with which the floor is paved, perhaps setting up vibrations. When nearly in position, the glass top shatters noisily, dramatically, into small pieces. The guy on reception hurries to see what the matter is. Edward declares his innocence, 'I was just moving it, it just broke on its own...' More staff come, with brooms and dustpans. We sit and watch. It's a relief when we can finally get into the car.

The flight from Ahmedabad is on time; it takes just over one hour, so we are in Mumbai by 11.00 pm. There, we have three and a half hours before setting off for London. Edward works on his book. I read Peter Carey. Of course, we cover for each other as necessary. 'Will you look after my things while I use the bathroom?', Edward asks. 'I will be ten minutes,' he adds, with informative precision.

Chapter Four

Karachi: More Time Out

In the snowy January of 2013, part of my job involves the Indian project. A sizeable delegation, most of whom we met in Gujarat, comes to London for a three-week study visit. To study under our guidance during the day, and to study shops and entertainment at other times. Their arrival is delayed a few days because some of the delegation had problems getting their visas in time.

The course gets going on the morning of Monday 14 January, with the usual introductions and explanations. In the early afternoon, I take a call from a solicitor who says that our house move is finally falling into place. Everything has come together suddenly, contracts are to be exchanged today, with completion in one week's time. My most urgent task is to alert the removal company and check they can work to that schedule. Which they can, of course, they are used to the stop-go of legal processes. I book leave for next week, and make changes to the course schedule to cover for my absence: fortunately, we are a big enough team.

After a few days of frenetic preparation, on Monday 21 January we are on our way, with our cats and our tons of clutter. A practical nightmare that is a story in its own right. I genuinely believe that I will never move again, that Spring Grove will be my forever home. We travel separately, so I can stay behind for the final clear-up. By the time I arrive, the doors are wide open to the cold, removal men tramping through snow, dumping things wherever they can. The telephone doesn't work, and it takes a couple of weeks to get it fixed: a massive problem for Mary's job.

Mary needs to attend events in London on Friday and Saturday, so on Sunday, we co-ordinate train times to enable me to meet her train at Darlington, pass her the car key, and catch my own train to London. I work on the final week of the course for the Indian delegation, and other things, then on Friday evening repeat the car-key handover meeting at Darlington, because Mary has another set of weekend meetings in London. Then I settle into a pattern of working in London from Tuesday to Thursday, and life becomes more normal. The great surprising joy of weekly commuting is that it does away with the misery of daily commuting. After breakfast, I just walk across the road from the Tavistock Hotel to my office, fresh, early and relaxed.

I have been trying to sort out when to visit the project in Punjab. Arrangements have been made, including flights booked, for me to go on Saturday 23 February, to spend a week in Lahore, and to fly from there to Karachi for the next TAKE Time Out conference. One of the consequences of our move is that it has halved the journey time to our house in Withernsea, from five hours to two and a half. We are there on Thursday 21 February. We are in Waitrose in Hull, a shopping break on our way home, when I get a call from Rosemary in Lahore. Straining to listen to the crackly line, among the vegetables with a full trolley, I learn that the trip is cancelled. Certain important people are no longer available next week. That's the reason the company is giving, anyway. This is life in international consultancy: everything is provisional, sometimes it happens, sometimes it doesn't. So I spend a week working in London, and go to Karachi on Saturday 2 March.

I leave London's Heathrow Terminal 3, supposedly at 8.15 pm, on a big double-decker Airbus, which is comfortable, quiet, smooth and reasonably spacious. The plane doesn't actually take off until 9.15 pm. One of the reasons for the delay is the need to spray de-icer over the wings and engines, and the captain helpfully shows this process on the screens, giving a commentary.

In the row behind me are two men. They are strangers, each travelling alone, but a conversation begins. The distance being so minimal, I have no option but to eavesdrop. One of the men is Singaporean, returning to Singapore. He is of the type who likes to speak to people, to know their business. He makes the opening remarks. The other man is British, heading for two weeks of work in Dubai. It is clear from his tone that he is more shy, reluctant to be drawn on himself and his business, but doesn't want to be rude, so says the minimum to be polite. The conversation continues, the Singaporean leading each step, offering information about himself, and seeking it in return. It emerges that they are both lawyers. Then, that they are both specialists in intellectual property. After a few more steps, it emerges that the wife of one of the men is currently giving technical briefing to the other man. How weird is that? If this was fiction, you would reject it as too improbable.

The airport at Dubai keeps getting bigger. This time I have to ride on a monorail to another terminal. The original schedule allowed over two and a half hours for this transfer, so the late departure from London hasn't caused a problem. The flight to Karachi is on quite a big plane (a Boeing 777) which isn't very full. The head of the cabin crew team suggests I might be more comfortable sitting in an empty area. As soon as I am settled, another man comes and sits beside me, which defeats the point of moving. He is a Pakistani going home, talkative, likes to know other people's business, whereas I am a shy Brit. Déjà vu. When he knows what I am doing, he says that his wife, who runs a school, might want to enrol in a future event.

The flight lands on time at 12.35 pm. I have only hand luggage and make reasonable progress. I can sense that it has been busy recently, and I am coming through as the tail end of a crowd is dispersing. As I come to the exit, I see that Taymur has come to meet me, and that there are enormous, happy crowds outside. The air is heavy with a delicious, intoxicating smell of roses. The flight before mine carried a returning Umrah party. Friends and relatives greet the pilgrims and shower them with rose petals, which are now lying everywhere like autumn leaves after a gale. The fragrant roses of the region are in a different league from those that grow in England. I would like to bury my face in them. In the car, Taymur shares his news. He has recently come back from the Middle

East where he has been doing something regarding the International Baccalaureate (IB). One of his contacts there, a woman called Mirna, has come to Karachi to lead an IB workshop. A number of the participants are coming from Saudi Arabia. My colleague Eleanore, who is leading the main conference programme, arrives tomorrow. We get to the Avari Towers Hotel at 2.30 pm, where I am greeted like an old friend. The very nice woman on reception says, 'You remember me? I am Pansy'. Pansy escorts me to my room with her usual pretty charm. I am on the 9th floor, with a wide view. A big red kite, one of hundreds, comes hovering and flapping just under my window, saying hello. of course, giving me a rare close-up view of a fine raptor. I am tired. I drink tea, shower and doze.

I go down to the foyer in good time to meet the others at 7.30 pm. State and provincial governments will be dissolved at the end of next week as part of the run-up to elections. Perhaps because of that, the news in the foyer is that there is a spot of trouble in Karachi, some incidents. This evening I am being taken out to dinner with Taymur, his wife Maliha, Colin, and Mirna from Jordan. Outside Okra there is a board which usually says, 'No photography, no staring, no cigar smoking'. This evening, I note two additions: 'No firearms, no politics'. So the election season is well underway.

I enjoy a starter of smoked trout and a light main course of grilled red snapper fillet with linguini. There are various other things on the table to dip into and share. The food, service and ambience are excellent. Taymur talks a bit more about the election. He explains that most of the votes are in rural areas, where communication is poor, and where many people think that Benazir Bhutto is still alive and still serving as prime minister. Whereas in fact, she ceased being prime minister in 1996 and was assassinated in 2007, six years ago. The current government have put her picture all over the place to trade on that ignorance. People in Taymur's circle are bothered that they might get re-elected. Taymur explains that when there are serious doubts that a government will allow an election to take place fairly, the army will step in and run the process, but that probably won't happen this time.

Monday is largely a free day for me. The two events are running not quite side by side. The TAKE Time Out conference runs from Tuesday to Thursday, and the International Baccalaureate workshop (which does not involve me) runs from Monday to Wednesday. In the morning, I hang around being sociable. The hotel's general manager, an outgoing Scot called Gordon, is bemoaning the loss of income caused by the local troubles. Foreign companies are pulling out their people: this happens every time. Some of the Saudis enrolled in Mirna's workshop have stayed in their hotel, even though they are at the Sheraton, which is only five minutes away. Public transport is not operating, and all the schools are closed.

Which is, of course, exactly what the terrorists want. The system dances to their tune, like a puppet show: exaggerated knee-jerk reactions whenever the strings are twitched. Massive impact and publicity from a couple of silly little bombs: that's value for money, a real return on investment, no wonder they do it again.

I can't help drawing a comparison with how the British public responds to terrorism: the best way not to give terrorists what they want is to ignore them. Carry on as if nothing has happened. In particular, I lived through the IRA attack on London in the 1970s. It was a bombing campaign designed for maximum disruption. Usually, warnings would be given to the authorities using codewords, buildings would be evacuated, and bombs defused. On a minority of occasions, the warning used a wrong codeword, or didn't allow enough time, or never got given. The effects of those rare occasions were by no means trivial.

In 1973, IRA car bombs and packages which exploded without effective warning in London caused 67 people to suffer serious injuries, mainly in Kings Cross, Westminster and Swiss Cottage. In 1974, there were four people killed and 145 seriously injured in incidents in parliament, the Tower of London, Woolwich and Portman Square. In 1975, seven people were killed and 75 seriously injured in a range of incidents. In 1976, 70 people were injured in just one of the attacks that happened that year, in a crowded exhibition hall in Olympia.

In each of these incidents and others like them, the scene at the place attacked would be like a war zone, and the effect on those injured and their families was profound. I am certainly not trivialising that sort of violence against civilians. My point is, however, that outside the zone of impact, no-one took any notice. On several occasions, I remember being in a bar or a meeting when a bomb went off some distance away, and someone would say, 'Oh, that was a bomb', and someone else would say, 'Yes that one was about a mile away I would guess', and then everyone carried on exactly as before. By comparison, I can't help thinking the widespread panic in Karachi is slightly unnecessary.

After lunch, I go with Taymur to the airport to meet Eleanore. We allow plenty of time, but when we get there we find that her flight is delayed, so there is time to kill. We can't go into the terminal, so Taymur guides me to Mcdonald's. It's not somewhere I would gravitate towards in England, but there is no option, and I am interested to see what it is like. It occupies the first floor of a brick building.

Two things strike me straight away. Everything is new, shiny and spotlessly clean. It is absolutely authentic, as a franchise should be, but even so, I am surprised by the detailed precision with which the brand has been recreated here. Background music, lighting, staff uniforms, every little detail: a perfect illustration of globalisation, and very useful for people who actually like the product. There are hardly any other customers. We sit at a table, which I scarcely dare touch in case I dirty it. Taymur has a large container of coca-cola full of ice cubes, and I have a large container full of watery black tea. After which, I am grateful to be able to use the pristine, globalised toilet, before we head back to the terminal. Eleanore appears, is happy to arrive in Pakistan, happy to see us, and happy to get some peace and quiet as soon as we reach the hotel.

I have a book with me for leisure reading. It is *Lady Audley's Secret,* by Mary Braddon, a Victorian melodrama first published in serial form starting in 1861. The focal point of the action is in Essex, but a strand of the story is set in another place which catches my attention. One of the book's central characters takes a trip there to unearth some damning evidence about the eponymous anti-heroine. In a cold January, he rides on a train from London to Hull, then transfers to a branch line, for a further half-hour ride to the fictitious seaside resort of 'Wildernsea' on the North Sea coast.

This can only be based on Withernsea, which at the time Braddon was writing, had recently started blossoming as a low-grade pleasure place for working-class day-trippers from Hull. That was made possible by the railway, a single track which curved its way through Holderness to Withernsea, where it ended at a turntable for locomotives. The railway was part of the economic lifeblood of the town, although as in so many other rural areas, it did not pay for itself once car travel became widespread. This branch-line was among the 30% of the national rail network recommended for closure in the report produced by Dr Richard Beeching for the government in 1963. Much of the route is still there as a bridleway which I walk along often. The track itself was torn up in a short-sighted act of official vandalism. The character in the story talked of watching, 'The grey sea slowly rolling over grey sand under the still grey sky. I should like to live here, and tell the beads upon my rosary, and repent and rest.' Yes, that view, that prospect in every sense, can only be Withernsea, I reflect, sipping tea on this warm spring afternoon in Karachi.

Taymur has organised that tonight's venue for dinner is a restaurant called Kolachi on the Clifton seafront. At last, I get my first sight of this strip of coast. The Clifton peninsula is oblong-shaped, poking out at a four o'clock angle into the Arabian Sea. Kolachi Restaurant is on its stumpy foot, in the middle of the short side of the oblong. As usual, I only learn that subsequently. Right now, dusk is just starting as the car reaches the coast road, and it seems that we are following that road a surprisingly long way. Surprising because I don't know where I am going, whereas you know that we are heading to the farthest point. We pass other restaurants, the sea looks RAF blue in the twilight.

We arrive and I am led into a world of breezy wooden decking, which is on several different levels, connected by wooden stairs made out of the same sort of planks, and populated with picnic tables of similar style. A big place in which wooden decking has turned into a landscape. It is busy, with noisy groups enjoying themselves. Battling with the sea breeze are hot gusts of appetising barbecue fumes. On the way to our table, we pass vertical decking planks providing windshields around enormous beds of glowing heat, in which are poked dozens of lethal-looking vertical spikes impaled with chickens, meat and fish. The smaller barbecues are probably burning charcoal, but the larger ones seem to be wood fires, of great logs that have reached the white ash-covered stage of maximum heat.

Our table is at the seaward edge – a prime position. I am excited by the view: not so much the view itself, because sea is sea, but by the fact of my being able to experience this particular patch of sea at close quarters. Typically, Taymur, his wife Maliha and Colin take no notice. Why would they? It is the air they breathe. Maliha takes charge of the food ordering. The menu is extensive, and the food is all good, and Maliha's hospitality starts running away with her. She is determined that Mirna and I should have the opportunity to sample dishes which she considers most enjoyable and most authentically Pakistani (because the menu includes a lot of international influences). She selects some, and, 'You must try this…and also this…' The waiter has to turn over a page to complete the list.

Moored close inshore is a small fishing boat of traditional local design. It is a sort of miniature dhow with high-pointed bow and a single small lateen sail. A long, impressive fishing rod is fastened in position. A fisherman is laying in the boat on cushions, his hands behind his head, his feet up on the gunwale, listening to a Walkman. The boat pitches and rolls a fair bit, and the sail flaps angrily. My first reaction to this scene is, 'Ooh how interesting, how quaint and traditional'. Then I realise the 'fisherman' is part of the décor of the restaurant: he has to sit there all evening to create atmosphere. As night falls, he is spot-lit. Other spotlights aim here and there, and it is strange watching seagulls fly through them. They glide along screaming, scarcely visible, then seem to explode in a puff of brilliant whiteness.

Food arrives. Prawns, large fish cut into slices, chicken cooked a few different ways, vegetables, rice, flatbreads and some accompaniments. I have a well-stacked plate and start shovelling it down. I like food, this is nice, and the breeze feels quite cool now, so I go at it with gusto. Then some more, then Maliha says, 'Did you try this one? Here, let me serve you.' As the meal proceeds, clearly gargantuan appetites are expected. A couple more dishes arrive, things it would be wrong for the visitors not to sample. I am past the shovelling stage now, eating politely, but aware that before too long I will be picking reluctantly. Colin, sitting on my right, wise old hand that he is, quietly advises, 'You'll find it easier if you always keep some food on your plate.' It works.

Tuesday is busy, with an early start, and the bustle of registration for the conference. Eleanore is leading the main three-day programme, which is about effective teaching and learning strategies to use in the classroom, while today, as a parallel activity, I lead a separate seminar with 18 headteachers on some aspects of school leadership in which they had expressed interest.

A year ago, Eleanore had pioneered the first of these conferences. She had explained various aspects of classroom practice which could improve learning. She had encouraged participants to design projects to carry out in their own schools, which would apply some of those ideas. She had worked supportively with groups and individuals to help them to develop those plans and had kept in touch with them at intervals over the year.

A central part of this conference now is hearing back from some of them about how their projects went. A number of groups and individuals have prepared presentations, including videos, which amount to a significant portion of the conference programme. Eleanore has achieved notable success, both in breaking down expectations about visiting Western 'experts' giving lectures and in helping to generate conference presentations by busy practitioners which reach an acceptable standard for this sort of event. More to the point, the participants thoroughly appreciate these presentations, made as they are by colleagues working in similar settings to themselves. A larger number commit to starting projects of their own. Next year's conference will be bursting with good material to report.

At the end of a busy, exhilarating day, Taymur drives us to the commander's party. As usual, his home is packed with people, refreshments and conviviality. The invitations are not extended to conference participants – that would clearly be impractical – they go to other people in the local education scene, and to the staff, trustees, patrons and regular supporters of our project. That still amounts to a good number, many of whom are keen to speak to the distinguished visitors from London. I pinch myself, being cast in that role seems an illusion. But then, much of an educator's life involves acting a part.

Not at all illusory is Taymur's mother, a successful fashion designer who cuts a real and striking presence. Light-skinned, with short, blonde-coloured hair, and a bold, flirty manner, I think it amuses her to bewitch me, and I am like a moth drawn to a flame. She is in full flight about the fashion industry, how any young person aspiring in it must be prepared to do the hard work, all the menial tasks in the workshop, before being allowed to design anything. She is casting herself as a dragon, a harsh, demanding boss, but somehow makes her regime sound like a delicious privilege.

Alcohol is plentiful at the commander's parties. Mirna from Jordan causes me to examine my stereotypes, which is often one of the benefits of travel. She is a Christian and enjoys red wine. She also presents as a very traditional Middle Eastern woman, with her black fully-covering clothes and covered hair. A reminder that culture, religion and westernisation are three independent factors.

On Wednesday, the conference is in full swing, productive, positive, impressive. The day ends with an extraordinary and memorable dinner party at the home of a young man called Zain. Apart from the commander's house, Zain's is the only private dwelling I ever get to see in all my dealings in Pakistan, and I am deeply appreciative of the honour. Zain is a lovely young man. He is handsome, charming, quick-witted, engaging and funny. A year ago he gave a lecture at the conference. Illustrated with many pictures, it was a provocative exploration of the interplay between evolving technology and traditional Pakistani culture.

Zain's home has a spacious, airy feel. It is not over-furnished, but the furnishings, décor and wall art on view have a decidedly arty character. Zain loves animals (perhaps that is one of the reasons I warm to him). He has nine outside cats and two inside cats, and various dogs. By 'outside', I should explain that the house has a securely walled and gated yard and garden, containing quite high-spec sheltered animal pens. I imagine this is a common set-up: the commander's Ridgebacks are similarly housed.

One of the inside cats, a white Persian called Chewy, is seriously ill, and Zain is worried and upset. It says something for his character that the dinner party is going ahead. Zain cares about his animals as deeply as if they were children. If any of them are ill, he involves the top veterinary consultants and spares no expense or inconvenience in pursuit of their well-being. For example, he has discovered a veterinary practice in Dubai which has world-class, leading-edge facilities, equipment and surgical expertise. His current anguish is because Chewy is too ill to make the flight to Dubai. We cannot see her because she is resting in a bath and not in a condition to receive visitors.

He does, however, introduce us to the other inside cat. He goes through a door and comes back cradling the cat on its back in his arms like a baby. He says, 'She is called Cobweb, from *A Midsummer Night's Dream*. She is a pedigree Himalayan.' Cobweb is beautiful, with bright blue eyes and long soft fur, and a gentle friendly disposition. Although slightly wary, she lets me fuss her. Now here is where memory plays funny tricks. I don't think such a serious cat enthusiast as Zain would have been wrong about the breed - that is unlikely. Himalayans are usually shown as predominantly white with large patches of blue-grey. Yet for years, I have remembered Cobweb as a lovely blue Persian tabby. Which goes to show, as I know from appearing in a witness box myself, that things remembered clearly may, nevertheless, be remembered wrongly. I wonder what else in these pages I have remembered wrongly: probably quite a few things.

I can, however, be certain about the meal, because I kept the menu as a souvenir. Zain is keen to emphasise that the dinner party is all his own work: concept, prep, cooking and service. The point is worth making because most educated Pakistanis have assistance in the kitchen. We are a party of six: Zain, Eleanore, Mirna, Taymur, Colin and me. Zain cannot bring himself to address Colin in any way other than 'Mr' and his surname. As for most posh boys in Karachi, Colin is his former headteacher. Red wine has been breathed and decanted. There is also white wine, juice and soft drinks.

Zain serves each of us with a large plate on which a selection of appetisers is artfully arranged. He says, 'My aim is to bring nouvelle cuisine presentation to Pakistani food'. Actually, he doesn't say 'Pakistani' but the shortened version, which is no longer polite in England. We have kabab, samosa, and a dahi baray tower, with a couple of sauces. The food looks good, and tastes good, and is gone in a few minutes, which I spend appreciating the hours of preparation it required.

Between courses, Zain goes anxiously to check on Chewy. Colin privately opines that feline euthanasia might be timely, but Taymur, who knows Zain well, says it would be unthinkable. I was the same at Zain's age, and made a poor old cat suffer for far longer than I should have done. Older, one learns the trade-offs between love and kindness. The next course, which is the first of two mains, is grilled marinated quail in chocolate sauce. It is different from anything I have eaten before, interesting and quite pleasant. It reflects Zain's originality, wackiness and boldness. The second main course is a capsicum stuffed with mince, with pea pillau.

Alongside these culinary experiences, conversation flows. Among other things, I learn that Zain is interested in setting up a new sort of design college, which would combine design with practical craft skills. The dessert is a sweet nest of fried vermicelli, containing khoya eggs made out of solidified condensed milk, and topped with edible silver foil. It is delicious, pretty, skilful and original. Mirna goes to the airport - her work is done, she leaves tonight. The rest of us linger a while convivially.

I take the early slot on Thursday, lecturing from 8.00 am to 9.30 am, then Eleanore begins the complex process of drawing everything together and organising support for projects which delegates will undertake over the coming months. There is a fair bit to do, and we agree to cancel a session I was due to lead during the afternoon. Eleanore and I set off to the airport at 6.30 pm. Her ultimate destination is Gatwick, mine Heathrow. I will stay overnight in London, to take in a meeting on Saturday morning before heading home.

The terminal at Karachi is crowded. As often happens in those situations, members of staff hustle one through the crowds and processes at a tremendous pace, barging in, squeezing through, waving passports in the air. At check-in, things are done in such a slap-dash rush that I only narrowly avoid being packed off to Gatwick with Eleanore.

On the flight to Dubai, Eleanore and I chat generally. She likes using Gatwick because she lives not far away. Her house is in a tract of countryside where I went for cycle rides as a boy. I tell her a bit about it. So my mind is on that time and place, while my ageing body is somewhere over the Arabian Sea.

Chapter Five

Lahore: Rugs and Tigers

My delayed visit to Punjab, to work on teacher certification and licensing, is rearranged at last. I am taking Chris, who did the last visit with Ian, to provide continuity. When I came back from Karachi, I went home on Saturday evening, returned to London on Monday evening, and went home again on Thursday evening. This is an experiment: I am going to try flying from Newcastle. Because it's there, because it seems right to support the region I now live in. I go to Newcastle on Friday evening, to a hotel beside the airport, ready for a departure at 6.20 am on Saturday 16 March 2013.

A while back, in January 2004, I had flown from London's City Airport in the docklands to Rotterdam to attend a conference. That was when making such a journey was new and strange to me, but the particular strangeness was using a very small airport. Walking out on the tarmac and stepping up into a small plane, landing at Rotterdam and simply walking from the plane, through minimal formalities, out to the taxi rank. Gingerly exploring Newcastle Airport at the crack of dawn brings back that memory. It is tiny, facilities are sparse, nothing much is open. From the limited offer, I buy the kind of porridge which comes in a paper cup, to which a burst of steam is added, and which requires vigorous stirring with a flimsy plastic spoon.

I board a small plane operated by Flybe which will take me to Gatwick, where it is due to land at 7.55 am. So hassle-free! A really good idea to use the local airport. I am getting good views of northern England, and it is certainly quicker than the train. A very limited range of catering is offered. The only thing I feel like picking is another porridge. The first one was tiny in relation to my normal breakfast. This one is similar, except that in-flight hot water compares poorly with the steam machine in the terminal. I have a paper cup filled with a texture like half-mixed cement.

The flight lands on time at Gatwick. My flight to Dubai is scheduled to leave at 9.45 am, allowing a comfortable period to get myself sorted out. Through the formalities, progressing from domestic to international, and into departures, which seems very crowded. Some crowds are sluggish, some fretful: this one is fretful. Quite a lot of flights, including mine, are significantly delayed. I send a text to Chris on my old, non-smart mobile phone to let him know. We planned to meet up in Dubai.

Now, as well as being concerned about how disrupted my journey might be, I am hungry. My normal airport behaviour would be to get stuck into some serious breakfasting. But everywhere seems to have queues out of the door and tables packed with people - of a kind I don't particularly want to squeeze amongst. There is a Pret a Manger, whose porridge I know from frequent usage to be properly made and of excellent quality, and which would wipe out the experience of the previous two. So that is my stopgap solution, and I always think of today as 'the three porridges journey'.

Finally, and with great relief I am able to board the flight, although I have given up all hope of catching the connecting flight. I don't do much on the flight except doze and read an academic book, about some things I am writing about. The passenger next to me is a large woman using a very large laptop, in a way that requires her nearest elbow to be poked well into my territory for most of the journey. The scheduled arrival in Dubai had been at 8.30 pm, for an onward flight leaving at 9.50 pm. It is well past that when I land. To my surprise, passengers for the connecting flight are hustled through: there has been so much disruption it has been held. I meet up with Chris, and we land in Lahore a couple of hours late. A driver is there to meet us, but progress is slow because we have to wait a long time at an army checkpoint, so we reach the Avari

Hotel at 5.00am on Sunday morning. I fancy a doze, and work doesn't start until Monday, so I agree with Chris that we will meet for a late breakfast.

Chris is a very pleasant colleague to work with. Smallish, athletic-looking, handsome, he exudes self-confidence, decisiveness and energy. His sharp mind is quick to generate academic insights but equally able to offer a wicked satirical critique of the environment within which we work. Since there is total trust between us, we can enjoy merry gossip between solving complex problems. He has an unselfconscious boyishness, for example, enthusing over the Nutella in the breakfast buffet. Eying my plate, he says, 'Ian told me how much you eat: I thought he was exaggerating.'

We have a week to work with our clients in the Directorate of Staff Development (DSD) and to maintain our working interface with the project management company. I will be setting off home at midnight on Friday. Chris is staying until Sunday, and will use Saturday to write our report. The core of our consultancy, and our reason for being here, is a two-day 'visioning' workshop we are running on Tuesday and Wednesday, with the key people in DSD who need to take ownership of the project. The project being, as you may recall from Chapter One, to set up an independent body to introduce new systems for teacher certification, licensing and professional development in Punjab.

On Sunday afternoon, I go through some preparatory work with Chris. We are using the first-floor lounge area near our rooms. The member of staff stationed here looks sad if no-one is using the facilities, which as well as tables for working, and easy chairs, include a sideboard with refreshments laid out neatly. I have tea and biscuits to keep him happy. Also, by vacating my room and sitting out here, it is easier for the staff if they want to pop in to do anything to it. For example, they might want to apply some strong air freshener to the bathroom.

On Monday morning, we are in the company's office to begin the day's briefings with Rosemary, our main contact. She introduces us to Rubina: this is an interesting new development. Last August, Rosemary had said that DSD was expressing interest in the company employing a locally-based research assistant to support the project and perhaps to be based in DSD. She said it cautiously, in a sounding-out sort of way, predicting correctly that I would be a bit sniffy about that idea. I couldn't see the point, couldn't see it as a good use of the project's budget. My organisation - a global centre of expertise – had been contracted in as the source of technical assistance. I felt slighted by the implication that a locally employed research assistant would contribute anything that our own deep knowledge couldn't provide. They were not noble thoughts. With hindsight, I understand this was about DSD taking ownership and wanting someone on hand who could learn along with them.

Having been advised beforehand that the appointment had been made, I am determined to be welcoming. That is the dominant thought in my mind, to be welcoming and nice to the new research assistant. 'This is Rubina', Rosemary says, indicating a youngish woman traditionally dressed in hijab. 'Delighted!', I say, smiling, with hand outstretched. 'We don't shake hands!', she says. In my eagerness to welcome, I am forgetting one of the most basic rules of interacting with Muslim women. Later, she shows me some of the research she is doing: information summarised in diagrams and tables. She is not far into her research; these notes are similar to what one of my own students might produce at the same stage.

In the afternoon, Chris and I go with Rosemary to the Directorate of Staff Development, to re-introduce ourselves to Nadeem and his deputies and to discuss arrangements for the two-day visioning workshop which starts tomorrow morning.

At the start of the workshop on Tuesday, I feel it is a real achievement to have reached the point where we can have a conversation about the heart of the project with a significant group of managers within DSD. We start by presenting three international models: the Ontario College of Teachers, the National Board for Professional Teaching Standards in the USA, and the Teachers Registration Council of Nigeria. Much of the morning's discussion concerns which aspects of these models are similar to what is planned for Punjab, which aspects are different, and the features of the local context which influence the design of the Punjabi model. Then we run through some key concepts, including the distinctions between qualifications, accreditations of practical competence, and professional statuses, and seek agreement on three levels of professional status to be conferred at different career stages. So far, so good.

Back at the hotel, Chris says he fancies a gin and tonic. Ah! So he knows about the speakeasy. On my first visit to this project, a year ago, Rosemary had surprised me by leading me to this unlikely facility. We climb to the first floor - Chris knows the way - and pad guiltily along a corridor and push open one of the bedroom doors. Except it isn't a bedroom, but a fully furnished drinking den. The barman appears with a look of disapproval. How he must hate his job! He inspects our passports and serves our drinks, then goes back into hiding. We choose a table. There is only one other drinker, who completely ignores us as he silently gets his fix, as motionless as a waxwork. Chris's company lightens the deadly gloom of the place.

Wednesday's workshop sessions go well. We are into more detail now, looking at how to motivate teachers to engage in the process of developing themselves: what mix of incentives and sanctions might be appropriate. Whether and how to accredit readiness for headship, and the processes for setting standards, and for assessing individuals against those standards. We explore what wider functions the new body will have: influencing initial (pre-service) teacher education, publishing guidance, advising on policy.

Rosemary has been taken ill, she will fly to the UK tomorrow. Earlier, she had said she would try to arrange for us to go to the border ceremony at Wagha, perhaps this evening, but that will not now happen today. It might get rearranged for tomorrow. As well as Rosemary's unexpected departure, the company's regional manager, who had been around for the last few days, is returning to China. He is Chinese, based in China. For all practical purposes, Chris and I are our own masters for the next couple of days.

Back at the hotel, we wander into the shop. Perhaps the successful completion of the workshop, and our release from supervision, puts me slightly into holiday mood. I decide to order a suit from the shop. A placard says they can be made up in 24 hours, and there is an attractive range of fabrics. The manager is only too pleased to assist. I pick a cream fabric in lightweight cashmere, and order a three-piece. The manager takes down all the details, and takes the deposit, then says, 'I will bring the tailor to measure you.' He climbs a staircase to a gallery and disappears through a door into the shop's private area, and reappears with an old man. This is the tailor. He has a grey beard, is dressed in a white Shalwar Kameez, and reeks of stale sweat: his wrinkled skin is glistening. He says not a word - I assume, knows no English, but looks me over with a penetrating eye and a tape measure. He takes his time: a competent artisan. I know what the deposit was for because I have done this before elsewhere. That was the actual cost of the suit and the tailor's payment, all the rest is the shop's mark-up.

On Thursday, we work on refining the legislation and developing the briefing document to go with it. Some of that we do in the hotel, and some in the company's office. Rubina tells us that she has the tickets for the Wagha border ceremony, and towards the end of the afternoon, she tells us it is time to set off.

This is an exciting treat, a piece of pure tourism which is also a privilege. The three of us get into a car, Rubina instructs the driver, and we are like children going to the seaside. When from time to time there is political or military tension between India and Pakistan, the British television news often shows extracts of the border ceremony as a way of dramatizing the conflict. Those images on television are all I know of it, really. They show the border guards of both sides strutting around each other like warring peacocks, impossibly smart, stamping, high-kicking, and staring at each other with theatrically exaggerated expressions of aggression and contempt. Now I am off to see it for real. The ceremony is daily, but this is certainly not something that happens every day to me.

The border is about 17 miles east of Lahore, along a major road which then carries on a similar distance to Amritsar. A railway runs alongside the road. Before the partitioning of India in 1947 this was a major economic thoroughfare. Partition cast this apparently arbitrary border through the area of Punjabi language and culture, leaving a sizeable tract of it inside India. We arrive at Wagha, which is Wagah on the Indian side. More specifically, at a dusty car park, where officials direct every move, and we make our way to terraced spectator benches. We settle, and I wait expectantly – it is quite a little wait until the appointed hour – wondering how similar this will be to those televised excerpts and what it will be like to see it first-hand.

The view from this terrace doesn't include the close-ups and camera angles of television, and it involves seeing the whole performance through from first trumpet blasts to the final shutting of the gates, lowering of the flags and orderly dispersal. It is a well-practised performance: clearly choreographed collaboratively by the two sides. I remember being told, I think it was during my first visit to India, that after the show of aggression is over, each side takes turns to host the other to a tea party.

Now, though, it is all aggression and competitiveness. The Pakistani guards wear black, and they are enormously tall. The Pakistani army must trawl its very sizeable ranks periodically, picking out the giants who get posted to this duty. They tower over their Indian counterparts, who are dressed in olive green. Both sides wear a headdress, rather like a stiffened folded napkin, to give added height. There is a lot of martial music and shouting, stirring up the audience to show patriotic support.

The thing that surprises me is that the spit-and-polish isn't quite so perfect as I thought it would be. In this light, from this angle, the black uniforms look a bit scuffed and shiny, and not perfectly fitting. Goose-stepping is done with slightly bended knees. The high kicks, however, look record-breaking. These very tall men, with big boots and enormous headdresses, bend their left leg, lean their body back surely to the point of imbalance, and swing their right leg up into the sky. If I was an enemy seeing that happening in front of me, I would be alarmed.

It is Friday morning, my last day, and Chris expresses interest in going to the zoo. I am grateful to him on two counts. The zoo is very near to the hotel, in a park on the other side of the road, a short walk along. Not far at all, but symbolically a huge step. On this, my tenth visit to Pakistan, it will be my first ever trip out of a hotel without a local escort. Frankly, had Chris not made the suggestion, it would never have occurred to me that walking out was even an option. I ask the guy on reception whether he thinks we would be safe going there. His reply is interesting, sobering. He is encouraging, but makes it clear that no, he couldn't really say that we would be safe. There were always risks. Chris's self-assurance is comforting. We walk through the security barriers and into the Lahore street-scene of busy traffic, jostling pedestrians, and half-finished roadworks. We need to find a place to cross, and come to a junction with traffic lights. These small unfamiliarities make travelling a pleasure. We reach the other side, and the entrance to the zoo, without being robbed, murdered or kidnapped. I have local currency, the entrance fee is modest, our exploration can begin.

Now, this is the other reason I am grateful to Chris. I like animals, but for so many decades now, visits to zoos and farms have been family outings, primarily for the benefit of children, and I would feel embarrassed about visiting one on my own, as if people will think I am a bit weird. I don't know why really: that's just how uptight and self-conscious I am. With his boyish spontaneity and sense of fun, Chris has no such inhibitions. So I get to spend the morning close to some wonderful tigers.

The zoo was opened in 1872, it is run by the government, and has clearly gone through phases of modernisation which are ongoing. The newer areas are large enclosures, open to the elements (the climate here is just right for many of the animals) and with efforts having been made to create a natural environment. The older areas are reminiscent of the old London Zoo that I remember as a child: animals in cages. London Zoo had been opened in 1828 and had gone through various transformations before I knew it, and more again before I took my daughter.

Some modern Western visitors would feel distaste that the older style of cage is still used in parts of Lahore Zoo. It is worth remembering how much countries like Pakistan, which are not rich, do for wildlife conservation. In Pakistan, many schemes promote forms of local community management which protect biodiversity, including the Himalayan Jungle Project and the Palas Conservation and Development Project. Other schemes protect dolphins, marine turtles, Chilghoza Pine forests and many more. I have to admit that the traditional cages make the most memorable feature of the visit, simply because I can get so close to the animals. I like the whole range, but fundamentally I am a cat person and like big cats, especially tigers. There are quite a few here, including enormous white tigers. They are close enough for me to smell them, see their expressions, feel their heat and power. Given the chance, I would willingly kiss their handsome faces.

There are more in the modern enclosures, also lions and elephants. It is a big zoo, with an extensive collection of animals. The information on the signboards includes how much each animal needs to eat each day, but this is expressed not in calories but in the equivalent number of chapattis. A relaxing morning, it is easy to become absorbed in such a place.

Towards the end of the afternoon, I revisit the hotel shop to collect my new suit. It is ready, it fits. While it is being packed, I choose a matching tie, handkerchief and cufflinks set, which I have never worn. Meanwhile, Chris is trying on jackets. I need to look at rugs. Mary asked me to, to find some in pale colours that would go in our bedroom. I check with the manager that they can be shipped, and then the long process of selection begins: he wants to show me a great many, I am making his day. I choose three that will look good against our carpet. Then the manager passes me a marker pen and tells me to sign them on the back. This is to prove that the ones which arrive are definitely the ones I have selected.

I am beset with the feeling that I will not be returning to Pakistan, that this is an ending, a separation. That is partly fuelling this now-or-never extravagance. On paper, the project we are working on has a long way to run, but the documents we will pass over to them at the end of this trip give them the essentials of what they need to plough their own furrow. They won't want to be managed, especially not by representatives of the former colonial power. I can't say I blame them. It is illustrative of a broader pattern, and right now, I feel it is touch and go whether my job will survive into next academic year.

At midnight, the driver comes to take me to the airport. When we had been arranging this in the company's office, people said that midnight seemed very early for a 3.20 am flight. I remember some unpleasant scrums and prefer to have plenty of time. Normally I never check-in online for return journeys because it isn't practical. I have no easy means of printing a boarding card, and sometimes the webpage is not in English, or the signal fails at vital moments. On this occasion, however, I took advantage of the company's facilities to get my boarding cards printed off. As I have only hand baggage, I think this will give me a big advantage: I won't need to get involved with the crowded check-in at all. My 3.20 am flight arrives in Dubai at 5.50 am, then at 7.40 am, I catch a flight direct to Newcastle.

As the driver gets near to the airport, it becomes apparent that it is exceptionally busy. It takes a long while for the driver to edge the car forwards through a sea of other vehicles and people in the drop-off area. The forecourt is packed solid - only people with tickets to fly are allowed to go into the building. I squeeze through the crowds towards where I think departures might be. Then I realise that most of this mass of people and luggage trolleys is actually the queue to get through the departures entrance. This means manoeuvring inch by inch towards one small, railed aisle. The people who, like me, are eager to get in have only a limited regard for principles such as queuing, taking turns, and respecting personal space. Using trolleys as weapons, or direct body to body contact, they cut across in front, squeeze in, and push from behind. One has no option but to be a little assertive, to gently but persistently claim space and edge forward. Once through, the first security check is particularly undignified because there are no trays, so my jacket, which contains everything that matters, such as wallet, passport, keys, vital medications, has to go through the baggage scanner loose amongst baggage. There is a slight wait for the body scanner because the officials are challenging the man in front regarding his bulky boots. He lifts up each trouser leg to reveal prosthetic lower legs. By the time I am through, my jacket is a dishevelled heap on the floor some yards away.

Finally, I am through into the check-in area. Now my enterprise in getting my boarding card should pay off. I have only carry-on baggage, so I will go straight to passport control. Here an official asks me repeatedly for my boarding card. I show it to him, pointing out the words 'e-Boarding Pass' in big black letters. He turns me back. This doesn't count. It might count in every other airport I have known, but here I must go through the check-in process and be given a 'real' boarding pass made out of cardboard. Thankful that I allowed plenty of time, I stand in the queue, acting calm patience, among the jostling scrum. When my turn comes, the man behind the counter seems to be taking a long time and making expressions. Then he presents me with three, not two, boarding cards. As I remonstrate, he explains that my flight from Lahore to Dubai will be late, so I will miss the connection that would have taken me direct to Newcastle (which I had been particularly keen to try out). So I have been booked onto a later flight from Dubai to London, then a further flight from London to Newcastle. These changes have added a further six hours to my already long journey time.

It is a relief to arrive in the departure hall even though it is packed with people wearing expressions of endurance. There is hardly anywhere to sit, unless I want to squeeze familiarly into single seat-widths amongst families and their strewn baggage. There is only one information board, so whenever I feel the need to go and see if it has changed, I lose my seat. After an hour or so's delay, there are signs of activity around the gate desk. Knowing the kind of queue that will suddenly develop, I go and position myself near the desk where some other people have started gathering. An official has started placing metal lane markers and attaching the tapes between them. Too late I notice that he has constructed a ridiculously narrow lane, which neatly curves around the spot I am standing on so that I have been cut out of the queue. I put on my colonial mien, which sometimes works, and cut into it.

After an age, the plane gets off, and I wonder if I could have managed the connection after all, and resent that option having been closed off. In the event, their judgement is vindicated. After landing in Dubai, the long bus ride from plane to terminal, and the security routine, mean that the gate for my original flight has been closed. I have a good hour and a half to kill.

It has been a long sleepless night, and 'breakfast' on the plane was some very spicy, very oily, lamb mince. I wander through the shopping mall towards the food gallery area. Most of the facilities are of the down-market 'grab and go' or fast food variety, all packed with people I don't want to squeeze amongst. Ahead of me is the caviar bar and to the left, some sort of posh place. At its doors, young women seem to be advertising it. I can't catch what they keep saying. They are holding a picture of quite a nice looking breakfast and the only word I make out is 'smoking lounge'. I accost one of them with 'Is it all smoking? I want non-smoking'. She assures me there is a non-smoking area, and in I go, from one extreme to the other.

Here there is wonderful decor, gold-plated plates, impeccable service, leaf-tea with strainer, really nice bread with fancy butter, no crowds, and the best Eggs Benedict I have ever experienced. The turkey bacon (it being a pork-free zone) is sitting on a bed of spinach, on a nice small muffin, topped by a perfectly cooked poached egg with a good liquid yoke, and covered with Hollandaise of the authentic homemade kind: quite vinegary and the texture of custard, all presented with neat artistry. The breakfast menu comes with a fancy wine list. I note the name, Oberjine, for future reference. You get what you pay for. What I regard as normal, proper, comfortable, as-it-should-be living incurs spending.

Chapter Six

Delhi: An Ending and a Beginning

T he big Indian project has been trundling along. There was our workshop in Gujerat in October, and the London-based short course in January. Earlier, before I got involved, colleagues had produced research reports on a number of topics of interest to the participating Indian states, and delegations from the states had gone on a series of study visits to look at good practice in various places, including Finland and Thailand. The participating states have also been running their own projects to implement good practices, and have been writing their own reports about what has happened. Now the Indian organisers of the project are planning a final conference, as a grand finale of the project and to celebrate its successes. We are to be involved.

We have mixed feelings about it because of the awkward relations which have bedevilled this project, and because some of us suspect the celebration may imply a greater level of success than has actually been achieved. Edward in particular would, ideally, prefer to have nothing to do with it. The Indian organisers want to run a workshop to build on some of the ground covered in the London short course. It will be either one or two days long, and will be either just before or just after the conference. It is settled that it will be one day, immediately before the conference, and Edward will need to make the main input. His presence is essential. In the end, he agrees to do it on the condition that I am there as well and that I do all the main interaction with our clients and hosts.

As well as our delegation, a former colleague called Roger, who worked on the project before leaving to take up a post in Australia, will be coming and will give a presentation. The overall director of our organisation is also involved, and will give a presentation by video link. Nikki, who is the research assistant and de facto project manager, and who has done much to keep the wheels turning as smoothly as possible, will also be coming to experience this climax to her efforts.

I am sitting in her office now. We are talking about applying for visas. She is explaining that the system has changed, that now the India visa application form has to be completed online. This is disappointing news. I am an old-fashioned sort of guy and I am used to printing off the terrible form, filling it in, and taking it in person to the visa agency with all the accompanying bits and pieces. India visas are usually issued only for short periods of time, so I have accumulated quite a collection of them over recent years.

Sensing my reaction, Nikki offers to fill in the form for me, here and now – she does things straight away – and has already got it on her screen. I am pleased and touched by this kindness, but also embarrassed because this is way outside her duties. She asks questions; her tiny fingers dance over the keys so quickly I can't see them. I think she is enjoying showing how quick and easy the task is. Certainly, she seems happily engaged. We get to the part which asks about 'distinguishing features'. I don't have any. 'None', I say: that is what I always put on forms. 'Oh, I think we should put something there', Nikki opines, studying me for a second. 'I am saying you have hazel eyes!', she declares, pleased to have completed all the boxes.

I am seriously bothered about some of the tasks outstanding in relation to this project. In particular, there is a report which I should have finished by now, but in truth, I am not sure I have all the material needed to complete it, and I have been putting off the problem of composing something which will look complete, using all the scraps I can muster. Perhaps I will get a chance to work on it in Delhi. I don't expect you to believe that since I don't myself.

Our preparations for the trip are well underway. A new post has been created in my department, and I decide to apply for it. It is a long shot, but I don't see why I should just roll over and not even try. It transpires that two candidates are short-listed: myself and an external, and the date for the interviews is the same date as the pre-conference workshop. I explain the situation to my colleague Gordon, who kindly offers to make himself available to help Edward with the workshop. I check that out with our Indian clients, who are very helpful and accommodating. That is that, I think, I shan't be going to Delhi. The project team here in the university take a different view. They are not going to let me off as lightly as that. I am to fly out when my interview is over and join the rest of the delegation.

So on the morning of Thursday 11 April, I attend the job interview. Nerves assault me, my brain freezes, I talk before thinking, and all the right answers come to me after I have left the room. In the afternoon, I give a presentation to an assembled audience. Which goes better, because I know what I am doing, but it is clear to me that unless the other candidate is unappointable, I have wasted my time. I collect my bag from my room, take tube trains to London Heathrow's Terminal Four, and board the 8.45 pm flight to Delhi, at about the time that Edward and Gordon will be nearing the end of the workshop that I should have attended.

At 9.45 am on Friday, the plane lands at Indira Gandhi International Airport. This is the fourth time I have felt the gentle thump of wheels on Delhi's runway. Inevitably, the previous three occasions have crossed my mind over the last few hours. Especially the first, which was my introduction to exotic work-related travel in June 2007. Unexpected, amazing, and, I had assumed, a one-off. A very significant experience, enabled and closely supported by the British Council. I came back to Delhi in October 2010, again at the invitation of the British Council. My third visit was in February 2012, at the invitation of an organisation connected to the Indian government.

On each of these preceding visits, I had struggled to get my bearings within the teeming metropolis. I had a map, but I find a map's aerial view of limited help when one is being whizzed along busy streets, especially if I can't put my finger on my starting point or destination. My first visit was easiest in this regard, first because it was such a monumental event in my life that I had done some homework beforehand, and second, because I was lodged at The Claridges Hotel. This very comfortable facility is in a central location, by a roundabout midway between India Gate and the Diplomatic Enclave, so it was easy to find on a map. One evening I had, very bravely, used the map to walk on my own from the hotel to the Lodi Gardens.

My second visit was more disorientating. Then, like now, I was coming off a night flight, arriving a day late to join something that was already ongoing. From the airport to a Crowne Plaza Hotel, then straight away by taxi to an address I had on a slip of paper which meant nothing to me. Only later did I locate the hotel as being at Okhla, towards the south of Delhi. My third visit was even worse. The organisers had told us our hotel and work venue were both in 'Delhi'. Only when we arrived did it become apparent that our hotel was in Gurgaon, a town to the west of Delhi, from which we had a gruelling daily commute to the work venue which was on Delhi's southern fringe.

Today, as I come out of the terminal and get into the car sent to meet me, I am mindful that I hadn't expected to be coming, and have only scant information about the conference I am attending. Orientation is not such a problem this time. The car glides smoothly to Connaught Place, where I am deposited at the luxurious opulence of the Lalit Hotel. I take the long walk across its vast, shiny foyer to the reception counter. I have an interval settling into a room which could have accommodated our entire delegation. A neatly typed note is brought to me, informing me that Chauffeur Bhanu 'will come to report you'. As I walk out to the car, I savour Delhi in mid-April. Not yet the scorching brightness of high summer, but warm and sultry, with just enough air to stir the palm trees. The street traffic is the usual mix of modern and traditional, Western and local. Swarms of mechanised rickshaws in their green and yellow livery ply their trade busily, getting in the way of faster vehicles. I am driven the short distance to the India Habitat Centre to the south of Lodi Road, almost opposite Lodi Gardens, which is the conference venue.

It is becoming apparent to me that the organisers have spared no expense. This venue is the equivalent of the Lalit Hotel: a top-of-the-range global class facility. When I reach the registration desk, having trekked across an expanse of ice-like marble, it becomes clear that this applies to content as well as to accommodation. The conference documents are nicely printed in full colour on stiff cardboard. When I find the programme among all the other bits and pieces, I realise for the first time the scale of this event. The programme includes a tremendous number of distinguished speakers from India but also from the countries where study visits took place. There are big names from Finland and Thailand, and several from Australia. The UK is represented not only by the delegation from our university but also by speakers from the Government's inspectorate and from its national staff college, as well as experts from other universities in England and Scotland.

The auditorium is laid out in a table-based seating plan, so it is easy for me to find and join my colleagues. By arriving late, I have missed the numerous welcomes, inaugural addresses and overviews from people holding senior positions, and I am not particularly grieved to have done so. I have also missed Edward's keynote address, for which I would have liked to have shown my interest and support. As I squeeze in near to Gordon and Nikki, the session in full swing is with a speaker from Thailand, who is explaining a scheme in Bangkok which is new to me. It is interesting, I am learning.

Over lunch, I hear that yesterday's workshop passed off smoothly enough. I am sure there will be some final small issues and frictions, but at the moment, it seems there is a good chance this project will conclude with everyone's dignity and reputation intact. One of the other delegates from the UK, Tom, worked for a while at a university where for some years I was part of a consultancy team. We were based in different departments, and our activities connected only to a small extent, and our periods of association with that university overlapped for only a few years. Yet in a situation like this, a long way from home, such slender connections become magnified, and Tom and I chatted on several occasions during the social interludes.

The afternoon presentations concern reports of projects which have been going on in the Indian states, then after a tea break there is a keynote address by the director of our organisation, by video link. In the auditorium, there is a tangible atmosphere of expectancy and concern regarding whether the technology will work. Which it does, pretty smoothly. The screen is enormous. We recognise our director's office, where he is sitting in front of a laptop. It is never easy giving an important lecture to an invisible audience, but he does very well: clear, confident and interesting, and handles an interactive question and answer session impressively. An uplifting end to the day.

In the early evening, I am sitting at a table in an external extension to the hotel's bar, with a glass of beer, having an undemanding catch-up conversation with Tom. His current projects are interesting and unusual, so I am happy to listen, and he is happy to tell me about them. It is dark now, and the air is stirred by zephyrs. One of them carries the distinctive smell of bad drains. I take this as a reminder that beyond our little patch of opulence, we are in Delhi. I am about to say something along those lines, but I catch a distant, thoughtful expression on Tom's face and judge it is better not to disturb his reflections.

On the way to my room, I receive text messages telling me the outcome of the interview I attended yesterday. It is still late afternoon in London. One is from the chair of the selection panel, telling me that the other candidate was appointed, and expressing the customary sympathetic sentiments about my disappointment. The other is from Personnel, rather more formally offering me feedback. I had known at the time that I had performed very poorly, that the outcome was obvious, but until it is confirmed there is always the possibility of a pleasant surprise against all the odds, of the kind that sustains buyers of lottery tickets. In truth, I am relieved, because the job would have stretched my capabilities, because I live too far from London, because I am too tired to want a big new challenge. But no-one likes rejection, and I feel dejected, perhaps because I must accept that I am slithering towards retirement.

Saturday morning, and I have a speaking engagement at the start of the day. The presentation for it is on my laptop, which I take on to the stage to get set up before the formalities begin. A technician connects it to the projector. Then he says, 'I'll just back it up', airily sticking in a data stick and fiddling about. I express anxiety: I may be a bit over-cautious, but I don't really like people fiddling with my laptop and walking off with my intellectual property. 'We do this with all of the presentations', he says.

Later in the morning, Nikki tells me she suffered from a very upset stomach yesterday evening, that the hotel had called a doctor in the night, and he had given her three different remedies, saying, 'One of them is likely to work'. The day passes in a series of presentations from several parts of the world, and from several Indian states. Some are interesting, some more routine. The formal conference programme ends early, with a tea break at 3.30 pm, because in the evening there is a cultural programme and dinner.

There is some small wrinkle in arrangements for transport back to the hotel, which means the cars are more tightly packed than usual. That applies to the one I am in. I am in the back seat, with Tom on my right, and the space on my left will be for Nikki, who, diligent as always, is somewhat late coming out of the conference centre. Now, I have made up my mind that I will give Nikki plenty of space. First, because her insides may be feeling uncomfortable, but mainly because I think it would be in poor taste, and probably offensive, to be seen to take advantage of the crush to squeeze up against a younger woman. She comes out of the building carrying files and papers, concerned about being late, relieved to see the car. I beckon her in, saying, 'Don't worry, we will make room. I am going to squeeze up to Tom, we have known each other a long time…' Which isn't true, but he takes it in good humour as I make enough space for there to be daylight between Nikki's slender hips and mine. While leaning somewhat on Tom, I notice again the bad drains smell: the problem must be in this area also. Tom is staring fixedly across the street, perhaps he spotted a drain cover there.

I have a short period in my room before it is time to go down to the cultural programme and dinner. I switch on my laptop. When it wakes up, it tells me the exact words I don't remember, that something is not right, it might have caught something nasty, it advises that I run a clean-up procedure. Naively, I accede to that request and press 'start clean-up'. It seems to proceed rapidly, with lists of files flashing up and being systematically and thoroughly dealt with. This is taking far longer, and involving more files than I had anticipated. I make tea. Eventually, it is finished, I can have my laptop back. When I attempt to use it, to access all my familiar material, I find none of it is there. I have a piece of equipment which is totally empty, all cleaned out. 'Oh, we are doing this to all of the presentations!', the guy with the nasty little data stick had said.

I meet up with my colleagues in a large hall, dimly lit, with tables set out in cabaret style. Nikki is sitting on my left: she has been on my left ever since she helped me with my visa application, the layout of her office requiring me to sit to the left of her on that occasion. There are some official opening pleasantries, several courses of food, and then a display of Indian dancing. The lighting gets dimmer as the evening proceeds. The dancers are young people, in striking costumes, with interesting music and dramatic lighting. The standard seems quite professional. I know that Nikki has significant experience of dancing, and lived in India for a period, so she is probably able to make a more knowledgeable assessment of what we are watching. I would quite like to ask her, but in this setting it is not really practical to exchange more than a few brief words.

Now it is Sunday morning, and I listen to interesting presentations about developments in Finland and Thailand, followed by a pair of lectures on the theme of inclusion. The first is by Tom, talking about a major project for which he is well known. Afterwards Roger, who used to be part of our project, talks about issues both in Australia and England, offering interesting and original insights. One of the points he is making about England is that life in the modern country today is very different from traditional images of English life: picturesque, 'chocolate box' England. To illustrate his point, he shows a set of pictures of green-pastured valleys with drystone walls and pretty villages. Which look exactly like Upper Teesdale, where I live. I can't resist turning to Nikki, on my left, and saying quietly, 'Actually that is like where I live'. During the tea break, I compliment Roger on his lecture, and he is surprisingly, touchingly humble. 'That means a lot to me, coming from you.'

The day proceeds to the valedictory session. The conference has been a success, and amid that general euphoria, discussions with our client about tying up the final loose ends of our project are amiable and positive. I am well aware that the loose ends do need to be tied, but I walk away with a sense of immense relief. Not so long ago, we were having serious, senior-level conversations about possible legal disputes and the risk of facing accusations of contractual non-compliance. The awkwardness and misunderstandings which had seemed to be such a feature of the project were certainly at that level, posing massive risks of reputational damage to our university. Never has a runner felt more relieved to enter the home straight than I feel now.

We check out of the hotel at 8.45 am on Monday and are driven to the airport, allowing good time for our flight which leaves at 1.45 pm. I check in for the flight with Nikki and we are allocated adjacent seats. Which is nice, but I wonder whether we will find much to talk about. Later I find out that these concerns had been reciprocated. I think of Nikki as a very able, efficient researcher and project manager: attractive, intelligent, willing and hard-working, and with a lithe and graceful way of moving her body around, but despite that string of qualities, I have not previously thought about her much as a person.

We take our seats: by strange coincidence, Nikki is once again to my left. Shortly after we are settled, Nikki, conscientious as always, makes the opening move by asking me my reasons for my career choice. I could answer safely, with the professional answer I would give in a job interview. I look at her eyes, attentive and expectant, and some imp, some demon, starts prompting me to take an enormous risk. I feel dizzy, this is madness. Her eyes are still expectant, inviting. She is waiting patiently. I have crossed a point of no return, and start spilling out the truth, things I never discuss with a living soul. I explain to Nikki about circumstances in which I found myself while still a teenager, and some of their dramatic consequences, in addition to the more mundane consequence of confirming my career direction. Nikki listens with full attention and interest. She remains supportive and accepting, non-judgemental. My panic subsides, the world is still turning, the plane is still in the sky. We find ourselves speaking frankly about life's journey, including some private things, in an atmosphere of friendship and mutual trust. This goes on quite a while. I can't really recall a comparable conversation, certainly not for very many years. I feel grateful to Nikki for offering me the experience. Cathartic and enjoyable and warmly privileged by the trust it implies. Within the weird cocoon of our companionship, I am no longer formal, uptight or shy. Everything seems different.

Nikki declares that after all this talking, she is tired and needs to sleep, but this seems to require her to make various preparatory adjustments in the search for comfort. First, she turns slightly towards me, while drawing up her knees, and finally her feet, onto the seat. I have seen this before: a particular feet-on-seat gymnastic that quite a few people seem to need to engage in in order to sleep on a plane. Leaning slightly against me, which feels nice, she appears to sleep. While feigning drowsiness, I am determined to stay awake so as to savour the present moment and the conversation we have shared. Thus the plane rumbles through the night, and only weeks later will my dumb mind and innocent soul twig that Nikki has been no more sleepy than me.

Grey dawn penetrates the cabin. We acknowledge that we are awake. With the efficiency she brings to all her work, she switches to a cool, business-like persona. I do the same. But in truth, I can't banish so easily the whirlpool of thoughts going on inside. Nikki's kind acceptance and support make me feel sure I have found a good new friend.

Landing, arrival, passport checks, baggage hall and customs happen normally enough. The delegation disperses, except that Nikki and I are taking the same tube train into central London. Now we are on our own, our conversation once more becomes informal. We are gathering basic information about each other. There is a woman sitting opposite to us in the tube train, observing this with interest. She is taking in our luggage, our work clothes, the fact that we have obviously just come off a flight. Also that we don't seem to know much about each other but are keenly finding out. I am pretty sure she thinks we have started an affair.

Nikki gets off several stops before me. I stand up and help her assemble her luggage. I take her hand and say, 'Thank you', imbuing those words with significance. 'No, no, I must thank you!', she responds. The woman opposite drinks in this tableau, no doubt assuming that these thanks relate to something of much greater significance than a conversation. After watching Nikki until she disappears from view, I sit back down and get out my reading book: a thick heavy novel. It happens to be Anthony Trollope's novel entitled *Can you forgive her?* As I hold the book up to my short-sighted eyes, I hear a gasping intake of breath. The woman opposite has seen the title, and is assuming I am showing it deliberately, reinforcing her misinterpretation.

Chapter Seven

Stockholm: New Friends

It has been nearly five months since I last left England on business. Worded like that, because I have had a short holiday in Scotland. Five months is long enough to set me wondering when, how, on what terms, and at whose instigation I will transition into semi-retirement. So it feels strange to be setting off again, like a reservist recalled to hostilities: this time to Sweden. Being a European destination, it has been hard to think of this as foreign travel at all. This will be the first time I have done a proper job of work in Europe. I went to a conference in Copenhagen in the very snowy early January of 2002, and took up the option of making a misty, gloomy excursion across the connecting bridge to Sweden, to visit a school in Malmo, where the students took decisions about how they would learn by debating and voting. I wrote an article about the trip. Then in 2004, I went to the same January conference, which on that occasion was in Rotterdam. That is the sum total of my professional exposure to the education systems of Europe.

There were some previous chances before I overcame my mental block about foreign travel, but I did not have the courage to carry them through. Sometime in the early 1990s, I managed to enrol myself on a funded study trip to Germany for education people, but the complexity of making travel arrangements, and my lack of German language, got the better of me. At a fairly late stage, I passed the place to my deputy, a much-travelled linguist. The same thing happened in 1998. A politician in the local authority I worked for organised a funded study trip to Belgium, his native country. With what I hoped came over as generosity, I decided it would be a good opportunity to give to my two deputies.

It is not vital for me to go to Sweden, as Joyce has led this project, but the organiser offered us two places, so I thought I should go as well, especially as in two weeks' time Joyce is going to TAKE Time Out in Karachi, relieving me of the need to do so. Only very lately have I felt any real involvement in or ownership of this project. That detachment has added an air of unreality about it. This is heightened by the fact that the flight allows only carry-on baggage, which means that my luggage is no different this week to my normal weekly commuting to the Tavistock Hotel in Bloomsbury.

The instigator and dynamo of this project is an interesting, personable and highly capable young man called Chris ('Chris S' to distinguish him from the other Chris in this book). He makes part of his living as a fixer of educational projects and study visits funded by the European Union. He has arranged for the UK delegation to travel together from Gatwick. As well as being a good organiser, Chris is notably confident and effective when dealing with groups: he has a definite stage presence.

On Tuesday 17 September I travel early from Barnard Castle to London for a day of office-based meetings, staying overnight at the Tavistock Hotel, where I enjoy a leisurely and very ample breakfast, not knowing where the next meals are coming from. I take a train from Victoria to Gatwick, passing through some old Surrey haunts, but so far as I can recall, this is the first time I have seen them from the train.

At airports I have a hellish compulsion to repeat my follies whilst disliking the experience of doing so. Then I sponge it all from my memory and do the same again. So at Gatwick, as usual, I arrive very early, and feel pleased with myself for managing to get my boarding pass out of a machine. So far, so good. Then, my mistake is that I have completely forgotten that I have been here as recently as March, when I had to hang around for a delayed flight, as well as on previous occasions. If I bothered to engage my memory, I would know what I am going to find on the other side of the one-way passage through departures. That does not happen because when I am travelling I enter a dazed, primitive, reptilian state of mind, focused only on immediate self-preservation. I imagine that once through into departures, I will find a spacious wonderland of comfort and convenience, where I may pass the time in scholarly reflection and genteel relaxation.

Through I go, into a hot seething mass of holiday-makers, many of whom look like the ones who don't book hotels because they will sleep wherever they collapse. Every seat is occupied, every walkway congested, and the shops sell things I don't want to buy to take away with me. Until about my thirtieth trip I wondered what sort of people need to buy this kind of stuff to take away with them on their holiday. Then I realised that half of the people here are going home. They buy gifts to take home. That is what the litre bottles of Scotch, perfumes and fine clothes are for.

I want to buy a bottle of tea and a cheap basic data stick, to put my presentations on so that if a foreign computer had something nasty in it, I will not lose a lot of material as I had in Delhi. These simple purchases are surprisingly arduous. After that I need somewhere to sit down, which brings me to the airport over-eating problem. The best prospect of a chair and reasonable peace seems to be Vin Rouge. There, notwithstanding a hearty start to the day at the Tavistock, I remember that I am still no clearer about where the next meals are coming from, so I have another breakfast, and pick the larger option because it includes black pudding.

When I can stay no longer, I wander around, hot, dazed and jostled, until I realise that I badly need another cup of tea. The most accessible tea seems to be in McDonald's, so, gritting my teeth at the indignity of it, there I go. The only place I can find to sit is at a long low table with toys that I think is meant for children. Then I find a seat in the central cattle-pen area and think about trying to write a few words. Joyce announces her arrival, we meet up, and she needs to eat, so back I go with her to Vin Rouge, surprising the staff with my re-entry. We are cutting it a bit fine. Joyce orders. I drink tomato juice. There is a power failure in the kitchen, causing anxiety; it is repaired. Joyce tackles her steak in the way we have to rush most of our work assignments, and we join Chris and the other delegates at the gate.

The project of which this trip forms the first main activity links a group of schools in a London borough with a group of schools in one of the municipalities in Stockholm. The headteacher and two or three other teachers from each of the London schools are coming on this trip to have a first meeting with their Swedish opposite numbers.

Joyce and I had agreed to use the flight time to catch up with some work discussions. While on the ground, waiting to start taxiing, we get going on a topic that involves Joyce in an extended and thoughtful exposition. Meanwhile, we are moving, safety announcements are happening, and we get onto the runway. For me, take-off is a significant moment. The plane gathers pace, I am clutching my stomach, taking deep breaths and staring fixedly at the passing ground. Joyce continues smoothly to argue the merits of a theoretical position as the plane roars and lurches into the air. As the ascent settles down and I recover my composure, I can't help interrupting to quip, 'that makes me wonder what else you talk right through.'

In Stockholm, the ever-competent Chris has organised a minibus to take us to the hotel, which is in a not particularly scenic suburb, the location of the municipality which is acting as host for the visit.

We check in at the hotel. I am disappointed to see no kettle or supplies of any kind in the room. Then we walk in a crocodile under a motorway along tiled subways that in England would stink of urine, to a station entrance and sort of shopping area: at least, I see a Co-op open. There is a cash machine that most of the others use to buy Crowns. I defer that decision for now: I want to get a better insight into how things will be paid for and how much cash I will need.

Dinner has been organised, and the one-course meal has been paid for, I think by the municipality hosting the visit. The choice is a veal escalope in breadcrumbs with an anchovy on top, which I have, or cod. It is preceded by a morsel of goose liver pate which I assumed was a chef's appetiser but I think is meant to be a starter. Some of the London teachers have not come across it before, and are amazed. Fortunately there are some conscientious objectors so I get a couple of extra ones. Since entering the dining room I have been waiting to see to what extent I should make conversation with Swedes. I am sitting between Swedish and English delegates and it seems fine to give my attention to the latter. I am next to a young woman called Jo, and on her other side is Clare, and opposite is Liz, their young headteacher, all three from the same school. Conversation flows well: light, jokey, easy and mainly professional and literary. I am drinking tap water so there is not an issue about my lack of local currency. Jo and Clare are matching my tap water with wine, and Jo wants me to agree to go out on the town with them on Friday night, but I will not. At the end of the meal they pay for their drinks, and when they do the maths, which is not so easy if you've had drinks, generally conclude that they were expensive.

On Thursday 19 September the alarm wakes me to a dark, cool morning of Nordic gloom. I turn the wrong way, hitting my head on the corner of the bunk above, then I remember where I am, and my lack of a kettle. Time is one hour ahead. The hotel is, I imagine, typically Scandinavian: clean, new-ish, nicely designed and minimalist, quite Spartan. The single bed has a fold-down bunk above and a ladder so neatly designed in that I didn't notice it until this morning. The shower is a bit awkward to use and is only half screened from the rest of the small bathroom, which has the thinnest plastic toilet seat I have ever seen. It emerged over dinner last night that some rooms have kettles, provoking envy. Fortunately, the tap water is cool and tastes like spring water. I have half a bottle of tea and some peanuts I brought with me.

Today there is a busy schedule of travelling on a train to the university and getting to know our Swedish links. A tour of the university is scheduled and various information exchanges. I am to do a session about leadership, and Joyce will lead another session and some interactive activities. I explore the breakfast buffet and try to work out which button to press for water for tea. I have to ask. The waitress points to a button marked Tevatter as if I am stupid. I haven't seen either a herring or a meatball yet. The breakfast platter is that nice mixture of warmish and cold on an icy plate (do hotels refrigerate their plates? How else do they get so cold?): smoked meats, scrambled egg, and a miniature mug of tea.

The English delegates gather and set off for Barkaby Station, which is near to the hotel, using a previously-issued card like Oyster to catch a commuter train to Stockholm Central. We have to wait for a particular train, and to get into a particular carriage, in order to meet up with the international relations person from the municipality who will guide us to the university. At Stockholm Central, we change amid commuter congestion and walk through confusing passages and escalators to the metro system, and catch one going out to Universitet. There, I am pleased (as only a geography teacher would be) to pass a *roche moutonee* outside the station. We walk through the outskirts of the extensive 1960's campus, which uniquely in the world is built inside a national park. We come to some grand oldish buildings which are the Natural History Museum, connected to the university, and on into the Institute of Pedagogics and Didactics, a name I think conveys Nordic Lutheran earnestness.

I do a double-take regarding the age of Sweden's education and parliamentary systems. Things got organised in the 1400s, and there were various important education acts passed in the 1600s. After we are settled in the room, I begin to feel better about the way we receive international visitors at my workplace. This room is arranged so as to be difficult to move about, with wonky chairs. There is a long search to add some tea to the coffee trolley, and then it is only herbal, green and other unpleasant varieties. After a lot of faffing about, our hosts think it is a lovely idea if we learn to sing 'incy wincy spider' in Swedish, with the actions. I am afraid I jeopardise international relations with my unenthusiastic approach to this treat.

We do the business. My session is fine, and the UK delegates are quite enthusiastic. Jo is pleasantly surprised, and I tease her for what that says about her expectations of me. Later in the day, 'We are your groupies' is how she puts it. For lunch, we walk to a campus cafeteria next to the museum. I am gloomy when I see an array of cold open-top cheese rolls wrapped in clingfilm, but cheer up when it turns out that we get a reasonable meal of cod swimming in watery tomato soup with salad. The best bit about the afternoon is that we are spared from the threatened one-hour tour of the university. When work is over, some of our delegation want to make whoopee in the town, but Joyce, Chris and I go back to the hotel. I extract 700 Crowns out of a machine on the way, to avoid destitution, which I think costs about £80. On the way back, I catch some glimpses from the train of Stockholm's very watery character with harbours, canals, and houseboat areas, with buildings rising steeply.

I have noticed a couple of exceptions to the general prevalence of good design in Sweden. The station signs are a fair bit higher than the top of the windows of the commuter train, so the only way to see which station it is, is to force your way towards a window, kneel down and look up at about 85 degrees. And doors open outwards into busy corridors, including the hotel rooms, so perhaps for the locals, the daily roulette game of whether they are going to be knocked unconscious adds much-needed spice. Joyce and I explore the hotel's dining, so the expense can be signed to rooms, and agree that it looks fine, with few other options locally. I have a smoked salmon starter and then a small portion of game casserole, in a pleasantly 'homemade' style with a small portion of rocket leaves and a pile of lingonberries. That costs an arm and a leg. Joyce and I share a bottle of 'cheap' wine and pay for that in cash to avoid complications: 350 Crowns.

On Friday morning, we are organised into small groups for school visits. Joyce and I are to spend the morning with Anna, one of our Swedish colleagues. In the afternoon, the whole party will assemble at the municipal office which will be the venue for some sessions, and I am to give another lecture. In the evening, we are to go out to an organised dinner in Stockholm Old Town. I have a streaming cold which is not ideal for diplomatic duties.

Anna takes us on a leisurely glide along empty roads. Instead of going straight to the school, she gives us the benefit of a guided tour. First, we stop at a very old church, where we get out to take photographs, then she takes us to see some quaint buildings that we would not have known existed so near to the drab environs of the hotel. She also shows us a residential area, including her own home. Although there is hardly any traffic and the houses are low-density, there is a fair amount of special acoustic fencing put in place by the municipality to reduce noise.

When we arrive at the primary school, it immediately presents contrasts to an equivalent school in England. It is open to callers: no razor-wire barricades, no electronic security. It is very spacious and sparsely populated, very well resourced, and has an informal, 'family' atmosphere. The curriculum is broad, and for a primary school, the range of practical teaching is impressive, especially what I see going on in a woodwork room and in a textile room. We meet people, receive information, and look appreciatively at things. I enjoy the school lunch, choosing from the reasonable selection a hefty frankfurter, good potatoes, and a nice salad.

Anna drives us to the municipal office for the afternoon. The English delegation like my lecture: I am not sure what the Swedes make of it. Jo continues to nurture good working relations. After we finish, Chris is hungry and dinner a long way off, so Joyce, he and I walk a short distance to a Wayne's coffee bar for a fish sandwich, a popular local item which I find quite pleasant and welcome as I too am hungry. Then we catch a train to the hotel, where after a period of free time, the party reassembles and takes a train ride into Stockholm old town.

I am engrossed in an educational discussion with one of the London headteachers called Evelyn, so at first I do not properly notice how attractive and interesting is the walk through the city centre. I regret that it is dark: there are attractive old buildings, it is clean, not crowded, and has lots of water. At first, the buildings are grand, reminding me of the Bank of England and its environs. Then we progress into a shopping district of old narrow streets, with attractive wares on display at impossible prices. There is a shop that just makes sandals. In the cheaper gift shops, furry bright blue and yellow horned Viking hats are on offer. We come suddenly to our destination, an Italian restaurant where the municipality is hosting dinner.

The table reserved for our party is downstairs: a steep climb round several corners, into extensive vaulted cellars, dimly lit and pleasantly atmospheric. We have a long table with seating either side. I find myself near an end, opposite our host, a senior official in the municipality. The Master of Ceremonies – actually, the waiter, but that is the part he is playing with great theatricality – makes a speech in heavily accented

English. He welcomes us to one of the oldest buildings in Stockholm, tells some stories about it, and explains how the set menu works: two starters and mains to choose between, and one glass of wine included, more available. After an unmemorable starter, I tackle the beef. This is a grilled slab, which makes one expect to find steak texture, but, in fact, it is sufficiently dry and tough to offer a jaw-aching challenge. It should have been carved into very thin slices. The Bearnaise sauce is good, the potatoes underdone. I would not dream of criticising a free meal, but our host (who has paid for it) feels less inhibited. The MC calls the gathering to order and makes an elaborate speech, expounding the incredibly high standards of customer care and satisfaction to which the restaurant aspires, and how on this occasion 'a little bird' has intimated that these have not, in fact, been quite achieved in every particular. He declares that panna cottas will be issued, notwithstanding that these are not included in the menu package. These arrive, two-tone pink and white, with various berries and trimmings.

By the end of the meal, Jo and Clare, who have been at the other end of the table, show signs of tipsiness. Jo repeats her insistence that I should go to a nightclub with them. I plead my snivelling cold and refuse. Some embracing occurs, and I take the opportunity to plonk a light dry kiss on her unresponsive lips: that marks the high water mark of intimacy. While hanging around for coats and toilet, listening to live music and singing, a number of women take photos of each other, only later noticing that they are posing by a statue of a naked young man standing on a plinth, which brings an unplanned juxtaposition into the pictures. Going up the stairs on the way out, Jo makes a final clubbing appeal and then says, 'But you'll come to our school and do stuff with us?' That is the real Jo. I promise, and keep my promise, although the 'stuff' turns out to be an unexpected and unprepared conversation with her class, of no great benefit to any of the parties involved.

It has been an enjoyable and relaxing evening. Except for Jo and Clare, and Chris, who is not staying in the hotel, the party walks back to the station and takes the train together. En route, I find out an interesting fact about Chris which explains his air of stage-confidence: I am told he was in the music industry and had for some weeks stood in for a well-known person as lead singer. We reach the hotel at about 11.30 pm but the group want to talk for an hour, making a late finish.

We are to assemble at 9.00 am on Saturday morning to catch the train to Jakobsberg for the final session of the programme. I rise feeling not as bad as I had expected given my cold, and late night: this is probably helped by only having been provided with one glass of wine at dinner. I breakfast at 7.00, and the eating area is brightened by a larger than usual presence of Swedish blondes. I keep spotting more and more of them, and they are joined by others. One fortunate man seems to be with, and in some way in charge of, about sixteen young women of similar age, appearance and mannerisms. They are made-up and animated with merry, girly chatter. About sixteen inches away from me, blonde hair falls freely over bare, sun-tanned shoulders; to the left is a double plait made out of buttercup stamens; and a number of high ponytails bob and swished nearby, while the man in charge tries not to look like a cat with cream. I wonder whether it is a company outing: beauticians, perhaps, or models. I can't refrain from commenting when Joyce arrives. She sensibly suggests it is a sports team: yes, of course.

The walk from the eating area to my room involves passing the toilets, the doors of which would, in English, be labelled 'male, disabled, female'. The middle one is labelled 'skotrum', and I misread it every time I pass. We have to check out and take our luggage with us for the day, and this gives a certain end of holiday mood to our party as we walk to the now-familiar Barkaby Station. It being a Saturday, we have to be especially let in when we arrive at the municipal buildings. The work programme proceeds well, including arrangements for the next stage of the activity in London in December. When it finishes shortly after midday, I have no clear view of what will be happening in the period until about 6.00 pm when we will need to catch a train to the airport. A personal issue has arisen for one of our hosts, who had planned to provide lunch at the meeting venue followed by some guided tourism, including a boat trip, but is now not able to do this. I decide I am happy to let others take the lead and tag along.

The group decide to take the train to Stockholm Central and have lunch there, and a consensus emerges that the best thing to do afterwards will be to go to Skansen, the folk museum on the island of Djurgarden. By now some of the group are showing the high spirits of children at the end of term, and locals on Jakobsberg Station are bemused by Nick (one of the headteachers) and the young women organising some panoramic group photographs in which some people run round from one end to the other so as to appear twice in the picture.

Stockholm Central Station is, at least to the nervous foreign visitor, a complicated mass of interconnections between the metro, commuter trains, the airport express and probably some other kinds of train, with shopping precincts and many exits to the street. The first job is to deposit luggage, which worries me because I like to clutch my possessions. For me to walk about a town without my briefcase feels much as others might feel walking about without their trousers on. I worry about security, about being able to acquire the right coins, about understanding what to do, and about ever being reunited with my precious baggage. I have never previously used a station left luggage system, but the left luggage system in Stockholm turns out to be a marvellous life-changing conversion experience.

For quickness and cheapness, insofar as that term has any application in Sweden, we lunch in the station, and small groups drift towards their preferred fast foods. I go with Jo and Clare and, for ease, point to their choice, which turns out to be good and surprisingly filling, mainly because the mountain of plain prawns is sitting on a hidden slab of pumpernickel which is spread generously with lard.

A small group around Chris act as the leaders, one of whom, Simon, has an ability to find his way in a foreign city that put to shame my credentials as a former geography teacher. I am happy to drift along behind with the flock. Simon's first miracle of navigation is to get us to SergelsTorg to catch the tram to Skansen. It is an ideal day for tourism. The sun shines on busy shopping streets, old building frontages and leafy bright green squares as the crowded tram snakes eastwards. Evelyn comments that the light is of a different quality in northern countries, and that some of the townscapes and waterfront scenes have a Russian flavour. I make wasteful attempts at photography through the tram window between passengers, then exchange standing places with Karen, who has nobly been taking up a windowless position right on the swivelling joint between the tramcars.

As we exit the tram, Jo asks me what my family and friends called me: is there a short version of my name they use? The truth is that in childhood, no-one shortened my name, and apart from during my time as a young schoolteacher, the only person to do so on a normal basis was my now deceased father-in-law. It is not something I encourage. There isn't time to explain that, so I offer, 'Sir, Professor, Your Lordship'. Actually I guess, correctly as it turns out, how Jo will address me in the e-mail that I know will come, and with what terms and symbols she will sign off. When it does, I remind myself that in modern social usage among some young people, these forms, while pleasant for a mature man to receive, are not to be mistaken for coquettishness.

The first thing we see when we get out at Djurgarden is some swirling dots in the sky that are people enjoying particularly high, furious, violent funfair rides. One sends them plunging to earth as if they are in a lift that has broken. As no alarm is raised, I assume that is just the impression. Simon leads us over the road to the permanent circus and up the hill alongside, looking for the entrance to Skansen. A woman dressed as a historical character, one of the museum's many living exhibits, tells us to go back down and further along. I am dressed head to foot in black Harris Tweed, and as the afternoon wears on and my gait becomes more old and tired, I see people look at me wondering if I am an exhibit too.

When I am in work social situations with a colleague with whom I have not travelled before, I don't know whether and for how much of the time they will want to operate as if we were a 'couple'. Some do, some don't. The party is straggled out coming down the hill. I come across Joyce walking on her own, and just at the moment that Jo is about to attach me to her and Clare, I sense that I should keep her company. At the museum entrance, we pool banknotes to buy a party ticket. Once inside, small groups want to separate. Joyce and I start by watching a demonstration of glass-blowing, which while interesting, is slower, more fiddly and less dramatic than I had imagined it might be. We look at other attractions including an ironmonger's shop, and its attached living quarters. Much of the museum reminds me of the Beamish Museum, for the industrial age, and the Weald and Downland Museum for older, rural features. I believe that both may have been modelled on Skansen, Scandinavians having invented the folk museum concept. There are some wonderful views. In one of these panoramas, I see a distant warship, which makes me wonder how, if at all, the daily life and culture of serving in the navy is affected by Sweden's neutrality.

One of the exhibits is a set of historic farm buildings, constructed out of massive pine logs laid horizontally, each fitting into the one below by a semi-circular halving joint. It is not the first time I have seen such buildings, but they have an interest for me because one of my going-to-sleep meditations used to be to mentally design and construct a log cabin using that technology. I never remember staying awake long enough to tackle the roof. These buildings are capacious, fitted out with exhibits, and tended by a talkative living exhibit keen to elaborate on the lifestyle of the period.

By this time, Joyce and I are keen to sit down and start to investigate options for tea. Having decided an open-air, stand-up kiosk style option is not good enough, we shortly come upon a comfortable restaurant that looks closed, but in fact is merely busy preparing for a function. We take seats at a table outside. Joyce has lager; I have two cups of tea. Jo and Clare wander into view, and find the way in, then out again to where we are, armed with large glasses of wine. We are nearly out of time if we are to re-group on schedule, and the young women show their facility with draining glasses. Our way to the meeting point includes a long and crooked downward flight of steps. I take my time: the handrail is a long way off first on one side and then the other. Clare kindly takes my arm, in a caring-for-the-elderly, practical, no-nonsense kind of tactility, and I play up to the part to avoid any misunderstanding. Jo decides to prop up my other side, to which kindness I respond with less reserve. Joyce insists on a photograph of me 'with my women', and takes so long fiddling with her mobile phone that I feel in genuine danger of pitching the three of us into a fall.

Back at Stockholm Central, and reunited with my luggage, arrangements are soon made for travelling by train to the airport. We say our appreciative goodbyes to Chris, who is staying longer in Sweden: he has been marvellous throughout. I am, by then, in the snoozy, zonked state that arises at the end of any assignment, however short and pleasant. On adjacent seats, Jo and Clare show the professionalism that belied their familiar, wine-drinking, fun-loving image. They have textbooks out and are planning workshops for a staff residential this coming weekend: every minute of the journey purposefully used.

At the airport, we have a meal, all squeezed around a circular table, and begin showing photographs. Jo shows me her puppy, and a cat conversation starts. A surprisingly large proportion of the group have fine portraits of their cats immediately to hand: I must get more organised in that regard. Jo is interested in where I live so I find a few pictures. She is amused that I order two mugs of tea at once: for people who like a potful and have limited time, that is just being practical. Both the meal and the tea are a good idea because we find that the plane has run out of refreshments.

Chapter Eight

Cartagena: Chocolate and Emeralds

I am leaving my house on the morning of Tuesday 8 October 2013. At the last minute I think it might be an idea to take a photocopy of my passport, which I do, and add the copy carefully to my travel papers. Just as I am walking out of the front door, I remember to go back and collect my passport from the bed of the scanner. It should have a flashing sign, 'Take your passport, you will need it!' I have hand luggage only again, which feels slightly risky for a trip to Colombia where I will have to speak to anything up to 1000 people under a spotlight. I think of things that might get spilt, through no fault of my own, such as by careless cabin crew. I have decided to pack a spare pair of trousers. In an emergency, a hotel could probably deal with a jacket, and I could be casual, but that is less of an option with trousers.

At Darlington Station, while waiting for my 9.26 am train to London, I buy a bacon roll from Pumpkin, with ketchup, of which I am given a generous two sachets. Out on the platform, sitting a bit sideways to balance the tea and roll, I am still thinking about possible careless spillages by other people, when I notice I am liberally dripping ketchup onto my trousers. Ah well, the smell is not that unpleasant and my black suit does not show stains too badly. In London, I go to my office, where

I have a meeting and a pile of 'must do' deskwork. That means I get ready for my journey in a bit of a rush. Just before leaving, I remember to check-in online, but then find I have not got my ticket with the necessary information. That must be at home somewhere. Because I am still at work, I can go through my e-mails and reprint the ticket: another narrow escape. The system does not, in fact, allow me to check-in online, adding to pressure tomorrow morning. On the tube to Heathrow, I eat my snack: good local Barnard Castle black pudding and bacon, but to be healthy, I have included a small lettuce and a whole tomato. Normally I do not tackle whole tomatoes. On this occasion, I set off some squirts of pips and juice in a nice pattern down my jacket.

Perhaps food splodges are not so out of place on this trip. I have been invited by the Nutresa Foundation to speak at a conference in Cartagena, Colombia. Nutresa is a global supplier of foods, especially chocolate, coffee, biscuits, ice cream, pasta and cold cuts. 'Things that make people happy', as Maria summarises it when I meet her. As well as this laudable service to humanity, Nutresa also engages in equally laudable philanthropy in education, including organising annually the event I am heading towards. It is the 13th Conference of Comprehensive Management of Education, and I have been allotted two hours to 'share my knowledge and expertise about educational change and school improvement'. I am gratified they think I have two hours' worth of that precious commodity, but mostly I am grateful to be given such a wonderful working holiday.

I have booked myself into the Park Inn Hotel at Heathrow, as I need to be at the terminal at about 4.30 am for a flight at 7.15am. I don't like it that the only practical way to get to Heathrow hotels is to go to the terminal and come out again, which is always tiring, confusing and sometimes expensive. The hotel reservation advised catching the Hoppa bus, which sounds so simple until you try to do it for the first time. What Hoppa, where, how? I walk to the exit from a Terminal, 2 or 3 it must be, where the central bus station is, and make enquiries. No, the Hoppa goes from Terminal 1. Back in for another long trudge. Really pleased with myself, I find the bus stop without needing to ask. A Hoppa is about to set off. No, says the driver, you need H2. So there are lots of Hoppas:

this is getting complicated. Eventually, the right Hoppa takes me to the right place, and I join a long check-in queue. I think I have paid enough to expect the hotel to have a few more staff on duty. By now, I have decided I am not relying on any complicated Hoppa-ing in the morning and book a taxi.

Early in the morning, I am swept along efficiently to Terminal 5 in a capacious Mercedes. I am too early: nothing is functioning. So much for needing to arrive three hours ahead of international flights. I am told I cannot be checked in for the final leg of the journey: that will have to be done locally. Through into departures, I begin to recognise the layout of the terminal. I look at Ramsay's for breakfast, but they are not opening 'for about 20 minutes', so I have a Great British breakfast at Huxley where I only have to wait five minutes.

The first leg of the journey, to Madrid, is uneventful. The dry brown hills and fields of Spain come into view. There are orchards of ochre studded with dark viridian blobs; these give way to red roofs, then industrial areas near to the runway. After the plane has landed, announcements are made at length in loud, clear Spanish, which I don't understand, and then repeated briefly in inaudible English. I catch enough to know that for the purposes of making the right connection, holders of certain boarding passes must leave by the front door of the plane, while others must wait and then leave by the back. This seems quite important, especially as there is not much time for making the connection. No staff are around to ask. I guess correctly, leave by the back door and have a bus ride to the terminal. Inside, all announcements are in Spanish, and while the surroundings are slightly familiar from a previous occasion, it is very confusing finding where to go.

I find the right gate, which is milling with people. The sign says 'boarding by groups'. Does that mean the parties of nine or more are to go on first? No, I eventually realise that this refers to numbers on boarding passes. All announcements continue to be in Spanish. I can't find a group number on my boarding pass, despite looking at it for a while. I find someone who points it out to me, and yes, I have to admit it says 'Group 3' in small letters. The problem is that I do not know what numbers have already been called. So I move forward. An official speaks to me sternly in Spanish, and I hear 'uno', in a tone that implied that I am unwelcome in any event, but especially if I am not in group uno. In clear firm English I ask, 'Has group 3 been called?' She snatches my pass, looks at the figure 3 on it, and says, 'Yes, that is group 1', waving me through.

The plane has no information panel on the seat back. I want to know how long the flight will be, and what the time is at the destination. I have departure and arrival times in both directions, so after numerous attempts at doing the arithmetic (only my reptile brain is active while travelling), I estimate that this leg of the flight will take ten hours and that Bogota is seven hours behind Madrid and six hours behind London. This means I am scheduled to land at Cartagena at 4.00 am UK time, 24 hours after I set off from the hotel this morning for Terminal 5.

I wonder who will occupy the seat next to me, hoping it will not be someone large, smelly, noisy or in any other way inconvenient. It is my lucky day. An attractive young Colombian woman claims the seat, who, above all other welcome qualities, is small and slim. She collapses immediately into a head-clutched-in-hands sleeping posture. I offer her my pillow to add to her own: she doesn't want it but thinks it is 'very kind'. Taking off, the landscape is greener than before, with large lakes that look as if they might have been dammed for hydroelectric power.

Eventually, a meal with an unappetising main course arrives. I dislike the lack of information about in-flight meal choices, which is usually limited to one ingredient. So British Airways might ask you to choose 'Chicken or beef?', without telling you that the former is mainly noodles with morsels of chicken, and the latter is a really hot curry. Usually, the airline will have taken the trouble and expense to produce a fully explanatory menu card; often cabin crews can't be bothered to distribute it. On this occasion, Iberia's choice is 'Beef or tortellini?'. The beef turns out to be unpleasant meatballs with the texture of frankfurters, tasting of artificial beef flavouring and monosodium glutamate, swimming in two liquids. At one end, gravy, and at the other end, completely liquid mashed potato. Nothing else: not a vegetable, just gloop.

My companion has taken lunch, and as tea and coffee come round, I decide it is time to overcome my shyness and attempt to improve Anglo-

Colombian relations. So my opening gambit is, 'I am English, so I drink tea!' A pause; I persevere: 'Are you Colombian?' 'Yes', she replies, 'I am Colombian, so I am drinking coffee. I don't usually, but I have a bad headash.' I don't hear very well, so asked what it was with the head: 'Headash'. 'Ah, headache'. 'My English isn't very good'. 'It is better than my Spanish. Do you have tablets to take for your headache?' No, but she would appreciate some, she thinks it would be 'very kind'. I feel very kind, empathising from my own unpleasant experiences. I start rummaging in my pocket, bringing out inappropriate things, and then get up to find tablets in my luggage in the overhead locker. She extracts two, but needs water, saying she will ask the stewardess in the distance. I can see that the stewardess is collecting rubbish, so that won't work. With a surge of fatherly instinct, I go assertively to the galley and help myself to water and a glass, which are appreciated as 'very kind'. I used to be the one who always had a sick headache when flying, and it is nice to get to a stage where I can help someone else.

We talk, briefly, because I think more sleep would be the best way for the tablets to work. She has been in Europe for two months on holiday, and is returning to Colombia for a family wedding. She lives normally in Miami. She started off in banks but now has her own business designing swimwear. I can picture her surrounded by beautiful people modelling her creations. I explain, briefly, what I am doing. She says that her mother runs a private school and might be attending the convention. Later, upon landing, she asks me my name and tells me she is Diana. Adopting a formal Spanish grace, she wishes me well and offers her hand to shake. It is long, thin, artistic, cool, waxy and completely lifeless. There are good views of the Andes as we descend into Bogota in the afternoon sun. More Spanish announcements happen, followed by a form of English, as part of which I swear the announcer says, 'We trust you have had a pleasant trip. We'll be a bit surprised to see you on your next journey'.

So here I am in Bogota, sitting in the cramped terminal for domestic flights, which has very few facilities. Not even tea. The best I can do after a lot of desperate gestures and crossly repeating 'Tea' with different accents, such as 'Tay', is to get a bottle of cold black tea with raspberry flavouring. One slurp and it is gone. Fortunately, I have some pesos about my person. The tea cost 3000: I am a big spender when it comes to pesos. I had thought that my long wait for the flight to Cartagena would be in the main airport, where there are facilities and they take Pounds Sterling (I forgot to bring dollars, they are also left at home), but the passenger flows didn't allow that. It was through customs, to a check-in desk, out of a weirdly uninviting fire escape door, into a bus, and here. It is just a holding pen: the way to the gates seems to be back out of the door and onto a bus. This is where I sit for at least two hours, some of which I fill by making diary jottings, notwithstanding that my laptop battery is running low.

For the final leg of the flight, I sit next to a father with two young children who scream, shout and racket around for the whole trip. I have not been to Cartagena before. My two previous visits to Colombia took in Bogota and Santa Marta. Like Santa Marta, Cartagena is on the Caribbean coast, about 100 miles or so to the south-west. Jamaica and Haiti are 500 miles to the north, and Costa Rica and Nicaragua a similar distance to the west. It pleases me to locate myself by reference to such exotic places, far removed from south-east London. Cartagena airport reminds me of the one at Santa Marta, small in size and facilities, but big in tropical vegetation. There is something pioneering and authentic about walking to and from aeroplanes across the tarmac. As usual, my major anxiety is whether I will link up with someone meeting me. I see a version of my name on a piece of cardboard: a driver, and nearby is Maria. She has done the practical organisation for the trip and had said she would meet me, and this is the moment to put the face to the name. She is lively and athletic-looking, with dark hair and a rosy complexion. In the car she briefs me on the programme, which includes an early start in the morning. She is staying in the same hotel, will meet me at 6.15 am to show me round, then breakfast at 6.30 am, and leave for the convention centre at 7.00 am, ready for the 8.00 am opening ceremonies. Given that it is already about 4.30 am in UK time, news of this early start is initially alarming, but of course, the extra hours mean I have a reasonable night ahead.

Once again, I find I have misinformed people about where I am staying. No hotel had been named, and I assumed the convention centre included accommodation. Instead, it transpires that I will be lodged at the Hotel Caribe. We arrive: it is a rambling place in Spanish style, spread across a large campus, including a tall-ish block for the main bedroom accommodation. Maria's room is nearby. Mine is extensive, with a long day-room/hall area, and typically Spanish in being dark, with much heavy dark wood, and in being apparently lavish but including very few facilities. There is some bottled water, and eventually I make the shower work – I have learnt that in some hotels you have to let the water run forever, and it will eventually come through hot - and that is all I need before going to bed.

I am up early and look outside. The hotel has white raised walkways with balustrades, masses of bougainvillea and similar flowers, palm trees and other sub-tropical vegetation, including what I think must be an enormous old rubber tree. These features, with the sunshine and heat remind me of Singapore. An ambience to luxuriate in, to feel thoroughly good about myself and life in general: an excursion to paradise. I recline on a sofa in the vestibule of the residential block to wait for Maria, who appears looking fit, eager and well made-up for the day's formalities. She escorts me through the fragrant garden to the main eating facility by the swimming pool, and I attack the hot and cold buffets of local fare.

The driver takes us by the coast road to the convention centre. Cartagena has a disproportionate amount of coast because it is built on an archipelago. I see beaches with palm trees and tents and notice pelicans flying along the shore. Just before we arrive at the convention centre, I see two reproduction sailing ships of the *Pirates of the Caribbean* era. Inside the centre, I am introduced to my hosts, Sol and Claudia, who are both senior Nutresa executives, and I am shown the main auditorium.

More than 800 people are milling about, predominantly female as is usually the case at education functions. Female beauty is aesthetically pleasing in any country. In Colombia it comes with very high heels, tiny skirts, acres of bare flesh from honey and cafe-au-lait to all shades of brown, and pleasantly rounded figures, combined with Latin vivacity, warmth, fondness for touching and cheek-kissing.

Focused on work as always, I enquire about translation arrangements.

Simultaneous translation will be provided only for my session. For the rest of the time, Maria will sit with me and be my interpreter. I am interested to see how this will go. I remember some delightful interpreters in Yemen, China and Mexico. It is really not so very bad spending long periods with an intelligent young female linguist pressed up alongside, whispering into one's ear. My concerns here are that in the last couple of years my hearing has deteriorated, that the English on offer is not that easy to understand, and that, despite the warm qualities described above, there is a formality and protocol about interpersonal relations which I think will rule out any close encounters. All of those factors do in the event prove to be obstacles, and I catch about one word in five, but it is easy enough to guess the general drift of the proceedings.

I meet Julio from the Ministry, with whom I worked on a previous project, and exchange pleasantries and goodwill. He is wearing the uniform that went with the project: a rugged jerkin that, in his case, is decorated with many badges. Lunch is, I am told, typically Colombian: a thick slice of roast beef, rice cooked in a sweet mixture alleged to include Coca-Cola, a piece of banana coated in something sweet and bright red that tastes like grenadine, and a bread roll. One meat and three starches, and no seasoning.

In the afternoon, I speak for an hour and a half, and answer some interesting questions to which I feel able to give challenging and controversial answers, which the audience like. I enjoy working with South Americans: despite the language barrier, I detect lively idealism and a sparky philosophy of education.

When my session is over, some young people appear and walk towards the front of the auditorium, and I am told there is to be a surprise. A band of teenage musicians start up with some lilting jazzy numbers. Many more join them, wearing distinctive costumes, then they are followed by dancers and the music changes to salsa numbers. The audience becomes animated, and a quite mature woman moves energetically to the part of the floor which has become the ballroom, partnered by one of the young performers. I am approached by another woman, so I exercise my well-practised manoeuvre of clutching my knee and explaining that my dancing days are over. The performers are young people who were out of school in a slum district, who have been guided and supported by an inspirational music teacher.

Over the next two days, I have many photo calls as groups of delegates wanted their pictures taken with me. I am accustomed to this, and it is no bother with such pleasant people. I put on my official fixed grin. The reason that many delegates want these photos is that they put them in their school magazines as evidence that the headteacher gets out and meets people. I am not under any illusions: anyone would do. As the crowd thins, Maria makes her farewell as she has urgent family business to attend to (I knew this – she had checked out as we left the hotel), and tells me that henceforth my escort (the minder variety, not the naughty sort) and interpreter will be Veronica. Veronica is a lightly-built, wispy woman in her early thirties, with skin the colour of manila envelopes and a certain kind of distinctly Spanish features. Her eyebrows, cheekbones, nearly black eyes, her lips and narrow chin could have come out of an Old Master painting of a Spanish aristocrat. She is quite shy, and her English is rusty, halting and very softly spoken. That notwithstanding, she is an attentive, efficient, thoughtful and thoroughly sweet companion with very pretty manners.

The arrangement is that she and I will be driven back to the hotel (she has been using the same room as Maria), where we will have about 45 minutes before going out again to a dinner hosted by Sol. I use the time to attend to work e-mails. Veronica emerges from her room in the same flowing blue dress, but freshly made-up and fragrant. Fortunately, the driver knows where to go. Quite often, when I am travelling, I am anxious that if stopped by the police and asked such basic questions as 'Where are you going? Who are you going to meet there?', I would have to appear suspiciously stupid.

The restaurant is in the old town, and is a particularly old building which has been lovingly restored to its current use, with a small hotel above, by its owner who is a well-known stylish fashion designer. I know she is stylish because her photo forms part of the decor, with one of her creations nearby. The old brick arches along one side of the restaurant are open to the world outside, or more specifically, to a pond surrounded by paving and gravel, backed by a high vertical wall of lush vegetation, which Sol explains has been created through an ingenious and intricate process. I sit on Sol's right, and on her left is her old friend and collaborator, Miriam, who runs her own private school, which Sol's children attended. On my right is Claudia, another senior executive in the company. Opposite me is Veronica, and on her right another woman whose name I never mastered. Thus I dine with five Spanish ladies (they are, of course, Colombian, and proudly so, but definitely towards the Spanish end of the spectrum in terms of heritage), and both they and I comment on this fact, and they decide that photographic evidence is needed, so we line up by the pond and a waiter obliges.

The restaurant is basically and recognisably Italian. Interestingly, whether on business in Sweden, Pakistan, Mexico or Saudi Arabia, or of course London, the safe choice is Italian. I choose a starter of baby octopus and a main of grilled fish, probably snapper: both on a similar bed of crushed jacket potato, with different trimmings. Drinks are discussed, and everyone gets a moderate, but in my case very welcome, slurp of white wine.

It has already been established that there is not much point in my sitting through all of the sessions tomorrow, and Sol has agreed to release me for a period with a guide so that I can see the old town and some other sights. Claudia is in the same taxi going back to the hotel after dinner, and she mentions the horse and cart rides as a good option. I immediately recoil from the thought of anything so obviously touristy, and am about to say so, but bite my lip, because Veronica is enthusing about that option. At the bedroom doors, Veronica takes a strong line that we should not start tomorrow until 7.00 am.

I fall into a welcome sleep. At 2.15 am I am awoken by loud clattering. I have been trying to incorporate it into dreams, and as I stir wonder if it is some loud construction work nearby. As I become more awake, I see that a storm is trying to tear out the windows of my sixth-floor bedroom. All are shaking violently, but only one is sufficiently loose-fitting to create such a worrying racket. Monsoon-strength rain is pounding at an angle, and spectacular lightning and thunder add further alarm. Palm trees are bent right over, with their crowns blown inside-out like umbrellas. Dozens of alarms have been set off. The immediate vicinity looks like scenes on news coverage of a hurricane. I am genuinely worried about whether the window will hold: that wasn't a literary flourish, and I wonder if it might be wise to put on a bathrobe. Sleep is out of the question: I just have to watch the spectacle. The storm blows itself out after an hour or so, as they do, and I sleep some more, but in the morning, it is still raining quite heavily.

I have not organised myself very quickly this morning, and it is Veronica who knocks on my door rather than the other way around. I am wearing a raincoat, with a hat in one pocket and an umbrella in the other. Veronica has not been to breakfast before and needs me to show the way. It is wet enough for me to put the hat on my head, and the umbrella over hers; she politely takes my arm. After breakfast, she wants to find a more direct route to the main lobby, and manages it with fair navigational instinct. There she needs to check out: I have another night.

I know there have been heavy showers, and there are some very big puddles, but it comes as a surprise that the driver has to keep fording major flooded sections of road. I have to be present for (you note my choice of words) the first session of the conference. On the way in, I am introduced to the president of the sponsoring company: a most charming man who has spent six years in the UK studying at LSE, and who knows Scotland and County Durham.

I settle down to try my best with Veronica's interpretation because I do not want her to feel inadequate. I hear very little, but guess some things to make a better show. She won't get really close, or speak up. I am straining, in the bending forward, ear-held-out, listening to interpreter pose, in which there is the issue of where to look. It is important not to inadvertently give the impression that one is staring intently down the interpreter's cleavage at close range. That is not a problem with Middle Eastern dress, but would be here, so I focus equally intently on Veronica's well-tended feet, where the manila skin is set off by brilliant, very pale pink nail varnish which she also has on her hands. In this painfully cricked fashion, we struggle through the session good-heartedly.

As I had hoped, the rain has rained off any further mention of horses and carts. We set off with our usual driver, who speaks no English. By now Veronica and I have established some conversational lines with which we are both comfortable, including the never-failing tactic of her asking me to give her some useful advice. She has shown me photographs of her parents, her sister, and of herself and friends at a salsa-dancing club; I have shown her some of Bloomsbury and Spring Grove.

The driver takes us to one of the many fortified sections of coast, with massive walls and cannons. This is where the guide will meet us. In the meantime, we walk around, taking pictures, and Veronica is obviously thoroughly happy to exchange this tourism for her regular work. At her instigation, the driver takes photographs of us together, with my hand around her shoulder and hers on ('round' wouldn't be practicable) my waist. It is all very chaste and formal, but that doesn't stop her bare shoulder from feeling very nice indeed. The driver, good man from first to last, obligingly takes quite a while fumbling with the camera.

The guide arrives: stocky, affable, almost a caricature of his role. He introduces himself as 'AJ' and sorts out the kind of tour we want. First, we go by car to the monastery on the highest vantage point, up a wooded lane with hairpin bends and white stone crosses at intervals, used in 'Stations of the Cross' devotions.

At the lower levels of this hill are shanty-like dwellings, which AJ says are without mains services, but are occupied by professional people because of their convenience for the city centre. When we reach the summit at 150 metres, AJ uses the views to explain the layout and history of the town. He explains that the building is the Convento de la Popa, built in 1607, which has doubled as a fortress at certain times. Then, in the cool interior, we see a courtyard, various exhibits and relics in a museum, and devotional facilities, including an ornate chapel dedicated to the Virgen de loa Cendelaria. The monastery and its surroundings seem to be covered with fragrant flowering shrubs flickering in the breeze. In the car park, a dog lays sunning itself as if dead; there are two donkeys for tourists' benefit – one miniscule – and a pair of hollow statues depicting a couple in historic 'piratical' costumes that tourists can pay to have their photographs taken with while standing inside.

Back down the hill, AJ stops to show us a sculpture of old shoes, commemorating a former city official who had used this imagery to describe how well Cartagena suited him. Street traders hassle us with trinkets and small craftworks of the kind that would have interested me in my teenage, pocket money, package tour days. Then we go to the old town which we explore on foot. This quaint and pretty district reminds me slightly of the old quarter of New Orleans, with its ornate, blossomed balconies, narrow streets, and variety of styles and colours of the buildings. Modern metal sculptures depicting the crafts and life of the city keep company with Simon Bolivar on horseback. Street vendors are everywhere, and the brilliant yellow national colour of Colombia is particularly evident because an important football match is taking place this afternoon.

We visit the emerald museum, which has a back section offering various dioramas of emerald mining, but which is in reality mainly an emerald shop. Colombian emeralds have a particularly strong green colour. The saleswoman tries to get me interested in a ring which costs $18,000 which 'would make a nice present to take home'. I keep protesting the impracticality of this. Veronica, to my alarm, tries on an engagement ring which costs a mere $1600, moving her hand around, catching the light, gazing covetously, and I have to resist a fleeting crazy impulse to buy it for her.

Later in the afternoon, back at the convention centre, it is time to say goodbye to Veronica and my hosts, which I know will involve courtly Spanish ceremonies. I deal with the hosts in order of rank, then moving aside a little, take Veronica's hands in mine and place a kiss on each cheek, take her shoulders and clasp them briefly to me, while uttering some fatherly inanities intended to be uplifting. All within the social rules. She comes out to the car with me, and feels it necessary to go through the first part of the ritual again. I wonder about the possibility of stealing a quick peck on the lips, on the way from one cheek to the other. Just wonder, but with amazing perception, she anticipates the plan and moves away: the rules of courteous kissing are strict.

That evening I dine alone, enjoying the hotel buffet. In the morning, wondering what useful work I ought to do before breakfast, I experience a migraine visual disturbance which decides the matter for me. After breakfast, I pass an unfamiliar bird calling from a nearby tree. I get a good look at it: it is brilliant, Colombian, yellow beneath, and blue-grey above. The shape of its beak, and general appearance, make me think of some kind of shrike. In fact, it is more likely to have been a flycatcher. The driver takes me to the airport, and as we pass along the coast, I notice flocks of egrets as well as the now-familiar pelicans. I have a fair while to wait for the flight to Bogota on which I am booked, so the check-in clerk puts me on an earlier one. Perhaps he knows something: in the event it isn't so much earlier after all. Going through security into departures I suffer a more prolonged and major visual disturbance. Fortunately, I don't need to see or read anything for a while, and by the time I need to walk over the tarmac to the plane, I can manage well enough.

In Bogota, I make a mess of finding the way from domestic to international terminals. I should have stayed inside, followed signs and got an airport bus. Instead, I come out, walk in both directions unsuccessfully, and very unusually for me, accost people for directions. In the end, I take a taxi for the short journey: it would have been a difficult walk. I check in and go in search of the food hall in departures. I must have been here twice before, but it does not seem familiar. I am surprised that the food hall in the international terminal of a capital city consists of a row of three fast food outlets. I choose Burger King. I linger over it, thinking I still have time to kill, but perhaps because of my migrainous condition (any excuse is better than none) I have muddled 17.00 hours with 7.00 pm in my mind, and idly looking at the information board for want of anything better to do, realise I needed to hurry to make the flight.

At Madrid, it is no less confusing than previously to find where to go. I also have to use the worst-designed security screening machine I have ever encountered. Unlike every other such machine in the world, this one has no surface or rack on which to place the plastic trays for the purpose of filling them with laptop, belt, jacket, toiletries, hand luggage etc. This is supposed to happen miraculously whilst walking along in a queue holding a stack of trays: they are to be filled without the use of hands, and then all carried, like an old-fashioned baker hefting a shop-full of loaves in a single load, regardless of the age or infirmity of the passenger. Meanwhile, staff shout at people stupid enough not to be performing this feat. I land at Heathrow at just after 2.00 pm on Sunday. My train north is not until 7.45 pm, because of engineering works, so I make my base in the Tavistock Hotel for a few hours. I enjoy a square meal, much tea, and its familiar environment.

Chapter Nine

Islamabad: City of Vision

There may be people who assume that the world of international consultancy runs with slick, jet-hopping, globe-trotting efficiency. Since getting back from Cartagena last Sunday night, I have had two days at home, two days working in London, and two days on holiday in Scotland. All fine, but right now it is Monday morning, with a long 'to-do' list, and I have been sitting for three hours on a stationary train stuck without any power between Darlington and London. Taking a call from Joyce telling me that her visa for Pakistan hasn't arrived and that no-one is currently working on a plan for how to supply it before the time of our flight to Islamabad, early on Wednesday morning. To counterbalance those worries, I have had two separate texts about my trip next week to Nigeria: one about flights, the original choice being full, and one to say my visa for Nigeria is ready for collection. As a seasoned veteran, I have achieved both a long-term Pakistani visa and the benefit of two passports, which enables travelling to continue to one destination while awaiting a visa for the next.

Now, on Tuesday morning, I realise that the list of things I had set myself to do is wishful thinking. In particular it was unrealistic to have planned to take part in my colleague Melanie's three-day seminar, Monday to Wednesday. On Monday evening that event enabled me to benefit from a pleasant Turkish meal and conversation in Bloomsbury. Now I realise, somewhat guiltily, that I will not be able to offer any other involvement, and Melanie will think I was just collecting a free meal. The work Joyce and I are doing in Islamabad is with a new client: Joyce took the lead in winning the contract and making the plans. The possibility that if Joyce's visa doesn't arrive, I will find myself performing solo is certainly keeping me on edge.

On Tuesday evening, I travel from Bloomsbury to Heathrow and feel positive about the comfort and familiarity of the Park Inn Hotel and the Hoppa bus. On the phone to Joyce during the evening, she reports progress: it all now depends on an agent telling another agent to tell a courier to deliver the passport to Joyce's home rather than to the locked office of the visa agency.

Early on Wednesday morning at Terminal 3, I find that my primitive old non-smart mobile phone will not make outgoing calls, but Joyce phones me, and to my great relief, we meet up, as she is now complete with passport and visa. The plane is a big two-decker Airbus A380. It is supposed to take off at 8.40 am, and gets going at 9.30 am. Not having flown with Emirates since my delayed flight and awkward connection in March, I am conscious of their slightly irritating features. They run tight transfers and insist on passengers arriving at gates well ahead of time, under pain of being shut out, as if passengers are only ever late because of their own laziness. But they themselves run late: to me it seems (although I know I was being unfair) quite frequently.

Our journey takes about 16 hours from boarding at Heathrow to arriving at our lodgings in Islamabad, where we will be lucky to get three or four hours' sleep before going on duty. This client, like many, has haggled over costs which have been cut to the bare minimum. When they see our schedule, again like others, they remonstrate: 'Why didn't you allow time to rest, to sight-see, to meet people?', and we remind them, 'That's because you wouldn't pay for any more of our time'. So it would have been nice to be able both to sleep as well as eat on the plane, but no chance. The thin complement of staff do everything so slowly.

After one hour, a tiny sachet of pretzels. After another hour, a meal. After another hour, clear the debris, and so on.

We have a smooth transfer in Dubai, and land nearly on time in Islamabad at 1.30 am on Thursday. I have hand luggage only, and Joyce has bigger hand luggage, so I assume that is it, but no, she steers towards the baggage belt, chiding me for my male unawareness of her need for several outfits. After an unbelievably long wait, she claims an enormous and very heavy case - almost a trunk. As we move to the exit, the powerful and pleasant smell of rose petals tells me that there has been an Umrah party returning. We are met by a very dapper young man with a loud tie and handkerchief set, who explains that had we come out earlier, it would have been too congested to move. He takes us to a small car driven by a maniacal young man, whom I have to acknowledge is both fast and skilled, insofar as none of the many near-misses become actual collisions.

As predicted, we get to our rooms at about 3.00 am, the time being four hours ahead of UK time. We are here for five full days of teaching, from Thursday to Monday, followed by a night flight out. We are lodged at the Islamabad Club, one of the few venues which satisfies the security requirements for British visitors. It is grand in scale and style and rather old-fashioned - it takes another day to get sorted out with plugs and internet – and both in ambience and style of operation, it is reminiscent of the Atheneum in London.

In the morning, I shower, handling the big, old, corroded plumbing with care. I examine the limited options available for breakfast and select what becomes my standard choice for the week: cornflakes without milk, a plain omelette, toast, and tea of creosote texture, made with three bags of Lipton's Yellow Label in a small pot. One of the first things I see outside is a green ring-necked parakeet of the London variety. Our clients have emphasised punctuality, and considering the shortness of our sleep, it is slightly irritating that the driver hasn't shown up. I meet Joyce and we are ready as instructed to be picked up at 8.30 am for a 9.00 am start but are still waiting in the foyer when the driver appears at 9.15 am, saying that the traffic has been difficult.

I try hard to maintain a sense of direction during the drive. The city has a completely different feel from either Karachi or Lahore. The guide book says that Islamabad was designed as a modern capital city in 1969 by the Greek architect Doxiadis. That name leapt at me: I had not thought of it for 40 years. In 1969 I had enjoyed a sixth-form work experience placement of a few days in the town planning department of Tower Hamlets Council. Whilst there, I had pored over, rapt by, a large book by Constantinos Doxiadis on the 'science' of modern urban design, which he called 'ekistics'. That 'science' was allowed its fullest flowering in Islamabad. The city has a pleasant and spacious feel, with plenty of room for expansion.

Eventually we arrive at the training venue. Styled a 'university college', it is the head office of the client's organisation, which is predominantly a large group of private schools. In this six-storey building, a range of post-school courses are taught, including the same University of London external degree course that Kiran teaches in Karachi. The space allocated for our programme is in the lower basement which usually serves as a recreation room, with adjoining snack bar for the students. The equipment is pushed to one side, including an enormous old billiard table which makes me think of the one in van Gogh's painting. Periodically throughout the day, students burst in boisterously before realising that their space for rest and relaxation has been requisitioned. Facilities are pretty basic. The two gents' toilets in the upper storeys for general use have no lockable door, paper, soap or towels. The one 'posh' one, which has these is outside the proprietor's office, and has a guard on permanent duty whose job is to unlock the padlock for people such as myself who are allowed to use it.

Morning and afternoon tea does not come with any snacks, as is the usual South Asian custom. It is, however, Lipton's Yellow Label teabags in Styrofoam cups, with an urn of hot water, which suits me well enough. Lunch on the first day is an incredibly oily, hot lamb mince, the effect of which limits my appetite in the evening.

The proprietor of the client organisation, called Walid, is a larger-than-life character: the archetypal 'big boss'. From other sources, I have been told that the business had been created by his mother, on a somewhat larger scale, and Walid had inherited his portion, the rest going to one or more siblings. He treats it as his beloved personal creation and all the employees as his children. Management of our programme at a more operational level is conducted by Urooj. She is the organisation's head of professional development and attends the majority of the sessions. There is also a young graduate who sees to all the day-to-day course administration, called Huma. She is diligent, obliging and speaks good English, having attended her primary school education in London.

The group we are working with is between 40 and 50, the number present varying from day to day. Apart from five men, the rest are headmistresses of various ranks and some younger up-and-coming female senior teachers. Later it emerges that all the participants have been hand-picked for the privilege of being in the group, even though they have to pay part of the costs themselves.

The men are shy, mainly bearded, studious, with a slight sharp smell of sweat. At tea breaks and other informal times, they tend to stay together, and like to engage me in earnest and respectful conversations. Meanwhile, at these same times, the women are like fluttering hummingbirds, talking softly among themselves, seemingly all at once, with many small, animated movements, setting wonderful fabrics wafting and glinting. Joyce relates to them as easily as I would have expected her to. She wears clothes of Muslim South Asian style, a different outfit every day, and the women appreciate this gesture to their culture. Joyce is of Nigerian heritage; she can wear these clothes with confidence and verve.

On the first day, about six or seven of the women are wearing a headscarf in the strict, tight style, with not a hair showing. The majority have more of a token chiffon drape or are bare-headed. The exposing of hair becomes more relaxed as the programme progresses. Unlike the men, the women are fragrant. Our programme includes table-based activities, and it is customary to wander around in a supervisory way, seeing that groups are on task, and dealing with any questions. As I do so, I am aware of the blend of fragrances and how this changes from one table to the next. Here is a table of sweet rose petals, here one of sharper, jasmine floral notes. There is a table of musky, spice aromas.

A group photograph is organised on the front steps of the building.

This has to take place at a moment when it is convenient for Walid to come and stand in the middle of it, and he finds it necessary to harangue the group about the importance of the occasion and to direct their smiling and gesturing.

At the end of the first day, it is a relief to get back to the Club. While Joyce investigates gym facilities, I make progress with obtaining an adaptor, as the sockets in the bedroom are of too old-fashioned a design to fit the adaptor I have brought with me. The Club is grandly proportioned, with massively high ceilings and impressive draperies in the bedroom. It suits me, notwithstanding that all furnishings, fixtures and fittings are 60 years old, and I am relieved that our client shows no desire to inflict evening corporate entertainments on us.

I dine with Joyce, or rather, I talk with her and watch her eating while I sip a very watery chicken broth, which is all I can manage. The Islamabad Club has some classic style notes. In the main ground-floor toilet near to the restaurant, there is an elaborate shelf with shoe brushes, big marble urinals, a pile of real towelling hand towels, and a clothes brush by the mirror. In the restaurant there are little wooden holders on the tables for membership cards to be placed. The menus handed to guests, ie non-members, are devoid of any prices: a nice touch somewhat spoilt by the fact that we have to sign the itemised bills at the end of each meal. The Pakistani Rupee has recently fallen considerably in value against pounds sterling, and it is almost embarrassing how cheap everything is.

It is common for people I meet on my travels to ask questions either about further study, or about getting into teaching in the UK. On the second day, Friday, one of the women wearing the full, tight headscarf, Beatrice, approaches Joyce and me to ask about teaching in the UK. We give her the basic information about the routes and systems for overseas-trained teachers.

Later in the day, she makes an opportunity to continue the conversation with me on my own. I repeat the information. 'It wouldn't work', she says quietly, her lip taking a slightly stubborn cast. In elaboration, she doubts that she would succeed in getting a teaching job in England that way. On the basis of all probabilities, that represents soundness of judgement. She wants a better option. There was something desperate and insistent in her manner. Finally she says, 'I want you to help me'. 'I knew that was coming!', I respond quite warmly, breaking the ice. 'Do you have money?' I ask, 'for example for course fees?', I add quickly, in case she thinks I am suggesting bribes. Beatrice looks happier immediately. 'Oh yes! Money is absolutely no problem. My father will pay anything required. I am a single woman and I must succeed in my profession.' I leave her with the suggestion that she consider applying to join a UK-based post-graduate teacher training course as a self-funded overseas student.

Lunch is chicken biryani, which is much kinder to my stomach. Power cuts take place frequently; as the training room is in the basement, it is plunged into pitch blackness. Everyone, accustomed to this fact of life in Pakistan, carries on as if nothing has happened. People have their mobile phones and iPads switched on, which serve as spooky lanterns. At the end of the session, Walid appears and makes a speech to the group. His speeches start off within the normal bounds, but moved by his own words, he becomes more impassioned. Undoubtedly he means well; undoubtedly he believes during his flights of fancy that his exhortations have positive impact. In reality, by about twenty minutes into his rhetoric he is contradicting the intended messages of our training, and being overbearing towards his staff in his words and manner. The group, clearly used to this, sit with an air of embarrassed endurance.

During his talks with me, Walid takes me to task regarding drone strikes that go astray and land on innocent people in Islamabad. I never know whether he is being serious or jocular. I protest that these weapons are American, not British, but he insists, 'It is your secret service which tells them where to drop them!'

During the drive back to the Club, I realise with a start that it is Friday: that we have worked through a long Friday without having made any arrangements for prayers, and without anyone having raised the topic. It being Friday, the Club's arrangements for dinner include a candle-lit buffet with live music, in a sort of ballroom, rather than in the normal restaurant. Joyce and I choose this option, with the consequence that dinner takes up more of the evening than we had planned. The live music is provided by one man on a keyboard, who also sings, and another man on drums. The numbers they play have a pleasant, light Eastern flavour, with long melodious phrases. We chill, hardly talking for long periods, savouring the sensuous blend of food, music, ambience and attentive service, and the good fortune of having a job which includes these benefits. Reality returns as soon as I am back in my room, where I deal with an explosively upset stomach, and an over-full e-mail mailbox.

On Saturday morning I oversleep, awaking from a vivid dream to realise that the alarm has been ringing for half an hour. Outside the front door of the Club are many plants in pots. As I make my way to breakfast, I pass a line of staff carrying some of these on their shoulders upstairs, to serve their turn as house plants. Each flight of the spiral staircase ends with a chamfer, beside which a notice says, 'Watch your step'.

Arriving at the now-familiar venue, we pass two of the cats that seem to live there, one black, the other a spotted tabby, and descend to the basement. In my youth, I fancied myself to be an amateur entomologist and took that hobby very seriously. When I enter the training room, a couple of men are chasing and stamping on something and misunderstand the nature of my interest when I say, 'Ooh! Is that a cockroach?' They block my view and kick it out of sight, embarrassed.

Beatrice has thought of some supplementary questions to justify further talk about teaching in England. 'This is important to you', I observe. With touching naivety, she explains, 'My father and brother have told me, they say I must talk with the tutors from England and make friends with them.' I emphasise that information and advice are the only forms of help within my power but agree that we will establish e-mail contact and that I will talk her through the relevant websites. She presses me for a personal e-mail address rather than a business one, and I refuse, saying, 'No, it is business', although in truth I use the same e-mail address for everything. I sense that she had been coached to make this request.

Lunch, as always, is served on the top floor, and a separate room is laid for Joyce, myself, and senior members of the client organisation. Staff fuss over us, bringing bottles of water and making sure huge amounts of food are within reach. Today's offering is a very oily dish of vegetables with chicken. After the group has dispersed, we are informed by Urooj that Walid would like a meeting with us, which inevitably involves our waiting on his convenience, to the point where I feel it necessary to ask what is happening. In he comes and we get down to business. Walid is keen to set up a continuing relationship. Both Joyce and I cut through his grandiose bluster to focus on the things that would need to happen in order to take his organisation in the direction he says he wants. In his office, stuffed with status symbols, we have a prolonged and seemingly productive conversation, for over an hour and a half, notwithstanding periods plunged into blackness by power cuts. We sketch out an option for continued collaboration; I set the price quite high, but after his initial problem with that, his interest continues. So keen is he that he urges us to lengthen our stay, and I take a quiet pride in explaining that I am committed to travelling to Lagos on Wednesday. As we leave, I think that, at least for a few minutes, he sincerely intends to delegate more, to invest in development, to continue working with us, and be open to advice. Back at the Club, Joyce goes to the gym and I enjoy my own company, dining moderately on fish and chips.

Sunday morning is dark and damp, with thunder and lightning. Strangely, the mountains are clearer to see from my window through the rain. In bright sunlight they are very hazy. Everything in the Club, including many small objects in the bedroom, bear its monogram. At first, I read it as a capital 'H', as that letter is written in cursive or copperplate script, until I realised that it was the 'I' and 'C' of Islamabad Club. Unusually, I feel a temptation, which I resist, to keep some small souvenir with this monogram: a sugar sachet, a wrapped toothpick, or a sheet of headed paper. Dressed in my business suit, I put toilet paper into one trouser pocket, and a small bottle of soap into the other. My false phone joins the paper, and false wallet joins the soap, ready to be offered up to any robbers with weapons. Thus equipped, I feel ready for whatever combat the day might bring.

It being Sunday, the roads are quiet and the campus is almost deserted. A few members of the group have arrived on time and more drift in. Beatrice is one of the early ones. I am sitting at a table looking through notes for the day when she comes to exchange greetings and pleasantries.

I notice immediately that her tight headscarf has gone. Not replaced with a less severe version, but gone completely, and her hair is not fastened in any way, but hanging full, long and loose about her shoulders. I can tell that she is self-conscious of the significance of letting me see her hair. It is nearly black, thick and shiny, and wavy: almost crinkly. I sit, looking up to my left. She stands on my left side, looking down to the right. As we exchange small-talk pleasantries, she runs her fingers slowly through her hair, down the right-hand side, as if tucking some of it behind her ear. Looking and smiling at me all the while, she makes a slight quick movement of her head, which causes her hair to move. Although it is small, and slightly awkward in execution, this move is deliberate and constitutes, albeit a minor example, a *swish*. Not only is she showing me her hair, and attracting attention to it, but she is even prepared to swish it, while looking at me out of the corner of big fluttering eyes. She carries out this routine in a shy, unpractised manner. How much she wants me to remember to give her information! How thoroughly, and, to be frank, successfully, has she applied her father's or brother's counsel!

The day's programme finishes at 4.15 pm, and I dine and gossip with Joyce, going early to our rooms to work. I go to bed at 11.00 pm, but loud music disturbs me until 1.00 am, by which time I have a headache, indigestion, and a sense of grievance.

Monday is the last day of the programme, and we will not need to leave the Islamabad Club for the drive to the airport until midnight, so Urooj has kindly arranged to give us dinner and show us some sights. The last part of the programme is for the participants to give group presentations. I give brief feedback on each presentation, doing my best to find positive things to say about all of them, and suggesting areas to develop. Their managers are somewhat inclined to put them down. Urooj criticises them for 'not stepping outside their comfort zone': a charge which Joyce stoutly and publicly refutes. Walid, in the course of quite a long speech, reinterprets my feedback comments as saying that one group has 'passed' and all the rest have 'failed'.

Then a course closing ceremony begins to unfold. This starts with the projection of a photo montage with a musical accompaniment. Next is a cake-cutting ceremony, in which Joyce and I have to pose like a bride and groom, with several other hands on the knife as well. The 'cake' is in fact a sickly goo of cocoa and cream. Whilst trying to eat this, numerous glass plaques are awarded to everyone who has contributed to the smooth running of the course, with a formal, posed photograph of each such presentation. Then the whole gathering is instructed to sit down again, and Walid invites certain individual participants to speak. They do so, and then more and more volunteer to add their own reflections.

Walid then launches into a second long speech himself, along lines by now familiar. Insofar as he has a discernible line of argument, it is to exhort the group to take more responsibility and initiative over vaguely defined areas of future strategic development whilst giving no indication of any intention on his own part to delegate decision-making or to renounce an iota of control. During this speech he demands attention, naming individuals whom he does not consider are listening fully. Some have transport arranged and are desperate to get away, the scheduled departure time having been grossly overrun, but Walid orders anyone trying to leave the room not to do so until he has finished. Finally, mercifully, he does so and the 'celebration' is over, by which time Joyce and I have missed the opportunity to see Islamabad in daylight.

Urooj extricates herself and, with Huma, we set off in the car. We are to dine at the Monal Restaurant, up a mountain road which climbs the Margalla Hills and leads to Gokina Moor and Pir Sohawa. The driver takes us crazily round hairpin bends, and makes several attempts at overtaking on the short, steep stretches between them, threatening head-on collisions with traffic coming the other way. It would have been a spectacular drive in daylight.

The slip road leading into the restaurant has a row of craft stalls, which we look at, but I do not want to buy anything. Huma, Joyce and Urooj want photographs of various combinations of our group, against various backgrounds. The restaurant is spread over an extensive area of mountainside, and offers a range of cuisines, but politeness precludes considering anything other than the Pakistani barbeque.

Urooj negotiates a table under an awning, offering a dramatic panorama of Islamabad. Immediately in front of us is a lower terrace of the restaurant with a similarly tented table. Beyond, mountain foothills make a dark 'V' shape, in the centre of which, as a broad inverted triangle, the city twinkles. We are looking south, or south-south-east to be pedantic: to the left, or east, the Marriott Hotel is brightly illuminated. To the south-west, and farther away, is a large, flood-lit building which Urooj tells me is the hospital.

A waiter takes orders for soft drinks. I have to avoid citrus fruit, so my preferred soft drink is ginger beer. No, they don't sell that, but they have a blue ginger beer non-alcoholic cocktail. They obviously get it ready mixed. He doesn't know what is in it but assures me it is non-citrus. When it comes, I don't share his confidence, but drink some of it to show willing.

Meanwhile, Urooj is organising the food. Pakistan grows wonderful vegetables, especially courgettes, carrots and maize, but they are rarely seen in restaurants, where the offering is usually meat, bread, rice and yoghurt. Urooj orders two kinds of chicken kebab, one kind smothered in cheese, which I have to avoid. She wants a chicken curry as well, and is really keen that we try her favourite, Chicken Achee. That name rings a faint alarm bell from distant memories of the days when I lunched often in Indian restaurants. I explain that I have to avoid things with a lot of lemon or lime juice in them, and ask her how it is cooked. 'Oh no', she reassures me, 'It is cooked in yoghurt, and ... er, spices'. I remember that professionally successful Pakistani women do not see their food being prepared. When the dish comes, the lime is immediately apparent, with wedges of flesh and lumps of peel as well as juice. I make a show of enjoying the rice and a naan, and a chicken kebab that is very hot and oily.

The next stop on our tour is a visit to the enormous and awe-inspiring Shah Faisal Mosque. We park and walk on a broad path of widely spaced, irregularly-surfaced stepping stones. These cross an expanse of what, in daylight, would almost certainly have been earth with scrubby grass, but by night offers an experience similar to picking one's way across a wide but shallow river. Notwithstanding that it is dark, and that we are at the mid-point between prayer times, we are not alone. Shadowy figures in small groups seem to float along silently in both directions. We reach dry land, so to speak, stepping ashore onto a forecourt area where the shoe-leaving station is located. This appears to be an open-air enclosure, haphazardly supervised by a single attendant, where shoes are left in baskets. My light slip-on shoes are the only footwear I possess south of Barnard Castle, and when I consider the consequence of losing them, my heart fails me and I beg permission to carry them.

We pad up wide steps to a paved promenade and a gently floodlit scene of tranquil beauty. Turning to our right, we stand for some minutes looking at the massive forecourt of the mosque, in the centre of which steps lead down to a square depression which is the ablutions area. A cat, exuding an air of spiritual ostentation, walks calmly across this. Turning the other way, we take in the mosque itself, with its geometric roof, mainly glass walls, and four slender minarets. Approaching it to view the dimly lit interior, we see notices that say 'Do not touch the glass', and many fingerprints showing the rule has been broken.

The final stop on our tour is a tea-room, its name translating literally as 'tea space'. This cafe has a menu listing dozens of fine leaf teas, and, just as welcome, a toilet. I choose a pot of Lapsang Souchong, and feel more relaxed than I have done for quite a while. The toilet is very publicly positioned, with a latticework door that is only one-third of the height of the doorframe, but needs must. After this, the driver begins the drop-off process, going first to Urooj's house, and then Huma's. After dropping Urooj, the conversation turns to London, and it emerges that the three of us, Huma, Joyce and I, have good knowledge (in all cases a bit out of date) of the East Ham area where Huma went to school. So as we are driven through Islamabad, we chat about East Ham and comment on living in a global village.

Back at the Islamabad Club, checking out requires no formalities at all. The same smart young man collects us, but this time he is casually dressed: I tease him about it. The airport is congested with a departing Umrah party. On the plane, both Joyce and I collapse into our exhausted states. I make the wrong choice for breakfast. When confronted with 'Cheese omelette or keema?', I attach too much weight to the word 'cheese', and choose what turns out to be a completely inedible oily mess of burning chilli, whereas the other option turns out to be a miniature

English breakfast platter, with only a hint of cheese. To make up for that, at Dubai I persuade Joyce to come to Oberjine so that I can enjoy the best Eggs Benedict on the planet.

After landing in London, I have to go straight to a meeting in the office. It is on a subject considered by other team members to require my chairing skills. I set myself up for such extreme scheduling because this particular meeting had to happen on a Tuesday, and if it does not happen today, it would mean my having to come to London on a day when I might otherwise work or relax at home. I judge it better to pile stress onto one day if that obviates the need to ruin other days. I am short of time, so spend money as necessary to catch the Heathrow Express, and a taxi from Paddington, arriving in Bloomsbury with an excellent demonstration of 'just in time' management. Had I not had the chairing role, I would have sunk into a coma in the first few minutes. As it is, I forget to put in my hearing aids until halfway through the meeting, but that isn't making much difference to anything.

Chapter Ten

Lagos: Encounters

After getting back from Islamabad, I spend one very welcome night at Spring Grove, arriving at 10.00 pm on Tuesday and setting off for Lagos at 3.30 pm on Wednesday. For speed and simplicity, I have decided to wear the same business suit, notwithstanding the difference in climate, so everything can stay in the pockets, and the only adjustment needed to my hand luggage is to replace used shirts and underwear with clean, and to replace my travel documents.

As I approach London, I begin to feel that a strange and pleasant transition is taking place. I am more relaxed and less bothered about the journey ahead. When, in something approaching panic, I first took proper stock of what my diary was telling me about this sequence of end-on trips, I assumed on the basis of experience that by now I would be too ill and tired to cope properly with the last couple of assignments in the bunch. In fact, to the contrary, familiarity and routine are at last paying dividends.

In the interests of familiarity, I have purposely booked into the Park Inn at Heathrow again, and catch the Hoppa with practised ease. I have a good dinner in the restaurant, and familiarise myself with which Hoppa to take to Terminal 5 in the morning. Having used Terminal 5 so recently, I remember what I will find in departures. Travelling later than last time means that I can enjoy the Gordon Ramsay breakfast, which is excellent. Towards the end of this meal, I receive a series of texts from Carol in Lagos, checking that I am awake and making progress. She is surprised that I am so well ahead of schedule, and I am impressed with the personal attention she is giving to the practical arrangements for getting me to her event. She is running quite a big conference and invited me to be one of the keynote speakers. She has booked me into British Airways 'World Traveller Plus' ('premium economy' in ordinary language), and I am looking forward to the rare luxury of the extra seat space this will provide.

That is about the only luxury that comes with British Airways' inhospitable regime. I am at the gate well ahead of boarding time and remain standing near to the assembly point. Fortunately I have only a compact 'pilot case' style bag. A number of people with only very slightly larger cases, well within the hand baggage limit, are accosted in turn by a BA official (I choose the word with care) and told they will have to put their bags in the hold because the flight is very full. They are put out, but have to do as they are told. This official then disappears, and when boarding finally happens, about 300 people with multiple bags way over the hand baggage limit are let on without objection.

Back at the gate, as boarding is about to begin, first by priority categories and then by groups of seat numbers, I am standing right at the front, watching screens to see when it will be my turn while a massive queue forms. Some airlines have the civilised system of separate queues according to the batches of seat numbers used for boarding. Another man has been waiting almost as long as me: we are, indisputably, at the front of the queue. Naturally, I and this other man have to move to one side to allow people past whose seat rows are called first. Then the man moves forward as his row is called, and is attacked by an official. 'You're *pushing in!*' she shouts, 'The back of the queue is *down there!*' (pointing to it about half a mile away). As the man quite rightly ignores her completely unreasonable outburst, she shouts even louder, 'Perhaps you should ask all of these people if they mind you *PUSHING IN!*'

I get settled: it is a good seat, on the aisle at the front of a block. The plane is an old Jumbo: an aircraft I associate with nasty sick headaches endured while crossing the Atlantic when I first started travelling again in 1999. The flight is due to take off at 10.35 am. It is still sitting on the ground at 11.30 am. A very long, slow taxi starts, while the estimated arrival time steadily latens. With rattling and roaring, the lumbering take-off happens.

After a while, tiny bags of pretzels are issued: I have tomato juice (plain, no ice) with mine as usual. Fifteen minutes later, the minor debris from this is collected. Half an hour after that, I notice that everyone is still sitting like lemons under their empty trays, believing lunch will be coming any second. It isn't. This is just one of the mean tricks that airlines use to prevent passengers from planning their time in usable chunks, and, of course most importantly, to prevent them from moving about. Lunch eventually comes, with the usual shouted one-word choices that give no information about the kind of meal that each option represents. At 3.20 pm, I note that everyone had been sitting trapped beneath their meal debris for over an hour, without a single member of staff visible. This, I assume, is to keep people immobile while the staff have an extended, jolly, chatty lunch break somewhere out of sight.

The route keeps close to the meridian, through France to the Pyrenees, over Valencia, to the Atlas Mountains and the Sahara Desert. It is so cold that for the first time ever, I unwrap the blanket and spread it over me.

At about 6.00 pm, the plane thumps down at Lagos and, savouring the humid warmth, I follow a trail of people into a terminal, which is a long, thin building with puddles on the floor and rows of buckets with rain plopping into them from a leaky roof. A notice explains that 'Terminal remodelling' (which could be interpreted in different ways) is going on. I come to an area with queues, uniformed officials and high-surfaced desks. There is a lack of signage and it is hard to know where to go. Only after I've got a bit lost am I made to understand that it is necessary to go to more than one of these desks: presumably one for immigration and one for customs. An official keeps very strict discipline regarding how I should stand. Following the throng, I come near to the exit, packed with noisy, jostling groups, and am delighted to see that Carol has come to meet me. I should explain that I have never met Carol before: we have communicated only by email and text, but it is obviously her. She is looking at me, smiling a welcome, and has an air of being in charge. This successful liaison is all very animated and a bit complicated because someone has been despatched to look for me around the luggage area, who has just phoned Carol expecting her to be able to tell him what I am wearing. Another passenger off the same flight, Tom, is also to be collected.

After a while, Tom, Carol and I, with a security guard, set off to find the driver. The guard is a bit of an anti-climax, or a reassurance, according to how one might look at it. A colleague of mine described landing at Lagos and being escorted between two fully accoutred warriors with heavy machine guns. This time the guard is a gentle-looking young man with no visible armaments, whose first instinctive action is to pick up luggage. I stop him, suggesting that I should carry and he should guard.

As we move along the curved frontage of the airport, amongst people and jammed traffic, over the uneven surface (the words 'pavement' or 'sidewalk' would be equally inaccurate), my main concern is to stay close to the others, to keep my jacket buttoned, and my arm where I can feel my wallet. We meet up with Carol's car, a Mercedes, where a side track enters the road. Tom, the guard, and I sit in the back. Carol, in the front, directs the driver in some detail and talks a lot, mainly about Lagos traffic and the upcoming event.

In the car's air-conditioned comfort, I take in the townscape. As usual, I have not had time to find out much about my destination: I tend to go, look, experience, and then afterwards try to work out where I was. This is my not particularly good way of coping with the frustration I feel at not being able to make spatial sense of unfamiliar environments. Adequate maps tend not to be easily available, and in any case, it is nearly impossible to orientate the aerial pattern of a map to ground-level views flashing past when you have no idea where you are actually being taken. The scenes I can see around me on the road, and the buildings passing by, are, apart from the people, similar to numerous other places I have visited. It is nearly dark, with the last of the day a band of coloured sky above the horizon as we start crossing the lagoon, which is definitely distinctive from other places. 'This is the longest bridge in Africa', Carol explains. The traffic coming in the opposite direction is heavily congested – almost stationary. Tom is saying what a good market there would be for a locally broadcast traffic congestion advice service that people could access through their mobile phones. All the way across the lagoon, the sky keeps flickering with what I would call 'harvest lightning': a kind of orange-coloured strobing without thunder.

The route crosses Victoria Island, and by a short bridge comes onto the peninsula where we will be staying, at the Eko Hotel and Exhibition Centre. This large modern structure, evidently at the premium end of the market, makes an interesting blend of internal and external space. Bedroom tower blocks, conference meeting rooms, and the main restaurant, are internal, enclosed and air-conditioned. The main lobby area, reception desk, conference registration and circulation areas, and some staircases, are roofed but with one or more walls missing, giving hot, draughty spaces with a predominantly external feel. Other circulation spaces, including what might otherwise be called a central atrium area, a bar, and the garden with its various facilities, are completely open to the impact of tropical downpours.

Carol checks me in. It is agreed that I will go to my room and then meet her in the reception area in ten minutes time and join her group for dinner. My room is some way up; an armed guard sits drowsily at the end of each straight section of corridor. I quickly establish that the wireless internet connection does not work, despite assurances that it does, and that there is no network available for my mobile phone, so modern communication is out for this short stay. Downstairs, I hunt around in vain for Carol, exploring lobby, reception, garden bar area. A violent tropical downpour is just coming to an end, with many intensely bright blue flashes of lightning. At first, I think this must be something man-made, such as a flashing ambulance or a firework display. Booming thunder and rushing wind complete the effects. Unable to communicate, and beginning to feel frustrated, I run into Tom coming the other way down a rain-drenched staircase. He decides we had best go to the restaurant, where we find Carol well into her dinner, and into conversation with two guests.

She airily joins us to the party, not at all bothered about having reneged on meeting arrangements. The other guests are Andrew and his wife, whose name I didn't catch: an English couple who run a school in Lagos. As conversation progresses I learn that Tom is half Nigerian, that he lives in West London where he is the chair of governors of a school. His day job is being an international entrepreneur and philanthropist.

Dinner is a buffet; Carol procures me a local beer. From the various food options, I choose tomato rice, a bean puree mixture, greens, fried plantains, and baked fish a little like mackerel, in a very hot oily sauce. When I get back to the table, Andrew comments, 'Ah! You've chosen local food. You'll know in the morning whether or not that was a good idea!' Tom seems to visit Nigeria periodically, and somehow the conversation gets onto how much Lagos has changed over the last fifteen to twenty years. Carol reveals, I think for my benefit, that her heritage is from Guyana (rather than Nigeria as I might have assumed), and someone had said to her that Barbados 'was like Lagos used to be'. As usual, I need to field the 'Is this your first time?' line of questions and to make a braver show of my African experience, which is limited to Kenya and South Sudan, comment that I will shortly be going to Ghana. 'Ah! Ghana is Africa for beginners!' Andrew advises me, 'Here everybody is louder and more excitable!'

Andrew has an issue about the billing of the drinks, because he says he has paid money at reception to create a pool to cover them, but that seems not to have been communicated to the restaurant. I leave the restaurant with either Tom or Andrew, I wish I could remember which. A member of staff is, I think, trying to check whether we have signed for the food. The one I am with explains, 'We have been with the party on that table over there, with the black woman. She has made all the arrangements about paying. So if you' (getting quite assertive, finger-pointing), 'have got any issues about paying, go and find the black woman and sort it out with her!' 'Yes, sir', says the man, unhappily. I find the exchange a bit uncomfortable.

The bedroom is furnished to a high specification, except that in the washbasin, there is no form of plug fitting, so one stares down an off-putting drain, and I remember the cockroach which had visited me by that route in Nairobi. There are frequent short power cuts, including one while I am in the shower.

Next morning, the humidity is apparent in condensation on the mirrors, and my clothes feel wet, including the waistcoat ('waistcoat?' I hear you say, 'In Lagos?'). I have a hardback book with me for light reading: Bryson's *Walk in the Woods,* and the pages are wrinkled as if it has been dunked. From the window, which I later orientate as facing west, the drawn curtains reveal an overcast, unsettled sky, over high-class buildings. Evidently, this is the superior part of town: between big, leafy dark green trees, the roofs and skyline suggest consulates, hotels and posh houses.

In the restaurant for breakfast, albums of sentimental love songs play pleasantly. I select various acceptable bits and pieces from the buffet, and make a special point of being polite and appreciative when offered tea. Earlier, a fat white man with a Dutch accent had barked out 'Tea!' in the tone of an eighteenth-century slave master.

After breakfast, I tour the grounds of the hotel, heading in a south-easterly direction, past the swimming pool, to gardens of lawns, shrubberies and trees, which are bounded by metal railings. Through these, I look across a quiet street to an expanse of calm water. This is not properly the South Atlantic, but the large lagoon of Karamo Waters. The sky has a dawn glow of pale orange, beneath clouds of gunmetal grey, and these colours are reflected in the water. I wander around a bit to see this scene from different angles and to check out the extent of the hotel grounds.

In good time I amble into the conference and exhibition area. At the conference registration desk, which is in a warm, open-air position, I am introduced to a young student called Folawe. She has been given the task of acting as my 'personal protocol officer'. Poshed-up and poised for her special role, a gazelle-like princess. She guides me through the exhibition hall into the conference hall and shows me where I might sit and leave my belongings. Then she guides me all the way back again to show me where to find the toilet. The gents' toilet suite is, superficially, of a high-grade modern design, but it takes a search to find a cubicle with a locking door, and all of the Dyson air-blade dryers have suffered extensive corrosion in the same place, under the user's left-hand fingertips. Folawe is waiting patiently outside.

The hall is filling up, and the conference begins with prayers in the evangelical style. These are followed by the Nigerian National Anthem, led heartily, passionately, by a booming male singer, with delegates joining in enthusiastically. Then a party of school children perform a play. The first plenary presentation is at a basic level: essentially, it is a sales pitch by an organisation that publishes books on the topics the presentation summarises. The second presentation is by Tom, which I find engaging and inspiring. It is about a scheme he is leading to identify gifted and talented children in Africa and to give them suitable opportunities. He has secured the help of massive global philanthropy and the support of numerous major institutions in Africa.

Andrew, who I had met at dinner, is the master of ceremonies for the day. During the tea break, Folawe seeks me out, dutifully to check that I have managed to find and drink tea. Of course she does not know that doing this is one of my particular accomplishments. Then she requires me to make a decision about where I am heading next so that she can escort me there, which seems to rule out my actual preference, which would be to wander about aimlessly.

After the break, for want of anything better to do, I sit in for most of a workshop session on school management, in which the speaker, in a thick Afrikaans accent, makes many references to the Bible, and to 'what God wants'. The overtly religious flavour of this (secular) education conference also appears in the words of introduction and thanks before and after plenary sessions. I also notice a lack of interactivity. Carol later explains that this is deliberate: 'If you open up the session to contributions from the floor, it will be impossible to stop people talking at length about irrelevant matters'.

Lunch is a buffet, served in the hall for delegates, and in a balcony area for speakers and guests. I gather a plate piled high with the local dishes and am guided to a place at a round table where pleasant conversation ensues. My speech is after lunch. Following the format of the other plenary sessions, I am escorted to the stage by a student who reads out a statement introducing me and giving my biographical profile. I copy previous speakers in thanking her for reading it so well and launch into my address.

When I have finished, and a thanking delegation mounts the stage to present me with a glass plaque, I notice that a new figure has joined the speakers' table, which is to one side of the hall. Big, beaming and important-looking in African robes, there is something slightly familiar about him. As I return to my place, he stands and shakes my hand, saying, 'Raphael, I came to hear you!' My mind is racing to identify him, he sees that happening, and after a second or two, he says, 'Yes, 'tis me, Tunji!' As recognition dawns, he gives me a hug. In a previous organisation and career phase, between about 2003-6, Tunji and I worked together on some tricky assignments in London. Now he is spending more time in his native Nigeria as a policy adviser. This encounter illustrates the problem of placing people when you meet them away from the setting in which you remember them. Also that links with one's home location pop up unexpectedly when one is far away. Meanwhile, Tunji explains, 'I saw your name on the notice of the event, and wondered if it was you, then saw your face on the website, so I had to come.' We set up a meeting in London, which duly takes place, to explore further collaboration.

Shortly after this, I need to start making preparations to depart before the roads become too congested. There is a slight hitch over financial arrangements: I had been assured that I would be reimbursed in cash for the costs of my visa. In the event, and with reluctance, bearing in mind how many financial scams are routed through Nigeria, I have to provide my personal bank details.

Carol comes with me to the airport. She decides to dispense with the security guard. This journey, in daylight, gives me better views of Lagos. We pass a congested, chaotic-looking market which Carol says is the best and busiest in West Africa. As well as conventional stalls, there are larger buildings of several storeys; constructions that seem to be made out of fabric, including a large Nigerian flag; and vans with their rear doors open, estate cars with their boots open, and absolutely masses of people. We pass a large area of shanty-style settlement, where the paths and gaps between the shacks are less than one metre wide. I wonder about the realities of daily life for the people there and think that it would take a brave westerner to go visiting.

A built-up area near to the main road has a mosaic of buildings, mostly three or four storeys high, with shallow pitched roofs, and balconies running the whole length of each storey. Despite those similarities, the buildings are of different colours and ages, and they are built at slightly different angles from each other rather than being neatly aligned. Masses of untidy telegraph wires and poles connect them. On a patch of open ground, right by the road, I see a group of birds that I note as 'mucky egrets': they are either very dirty ordinary egrets or a tinted variety.

On one stretch of road, there seems to be some cause of congestion ahead, and it appears that policemen, on the right-hand edge of the carriageway, are stopping various cars. Carol becomes extremely agitated, urging the driver, 'Don't look at them! Don't catch their eyes! Get right over to the left! If they try to stop you, just ignore them!' As we go past, and still very uptight, Carol explains: 'They are so corrupt! If they like your car, they will say there is something wrong with the registration and requisition it. They will say your papers are out of order and demand bribes to give them back to you.' She indicates some dramatic personal experiences along these lines and a willingness to fight savagely to defend her rights.

The roads are getting more congested, and the driver chooses a route beside expanses of red earth with scrubby grass, scuffed and rutted by vehicles. One area seems to be a depot or terminus for yellow minibuses. An area of rough, uneven ground is a packed car park.

As we get nearer to the airport, Carol adds more information to her personal background, explaining that really she is a 'Bromley and Beckenham girl'. I summarise my long connections with both places, and we discuss the school she went to and the school I taught in, which was regarded by hers as 'posh'. I mention that in my first year of teaching, I lived in the former fire station in Kelsey Square, Beckenham. It disconcerts me to learn that she knows that building well.

Acting on Carol's advice which I am sure, overall, was sound, I pay a

$50 entry fee to a Gabfol lounge at Lagos airport terminal, which can be my temporary home during the long wait until my flight is due to leave. When I go in, it is virtually deserted. I explore and get my bearings, being unfamiliar with such places. The money-extracting counter is in a restaurant area, and I go from there into the lounge. This is pleasantly empty. Getting in takes a few moments because I can't see anything which looks like a door. But I discover by accident that if you walk boldly towards a glass wall, it opens. I notice happily that there are plenty of power sockets in certain parts of the room. I have five hours to kill before needing to go to the gate for my flight, so this peaceful environment will be fine. The early arrival was considered necessary to get off the island before the traffic becomes paralysed. Even travelling when I did, the roads had been thick and slow with jostling, crazy drivers.

I make a phone call home, saying how nice and empty the lounge is, and immediately six big noisy men with a lot of hand luggage burst into the room and take the chairs near the power sockets. Not yet understanding that drinks and regular supplies of hot tit-bits will be freely available at intervals in this lounge area (well, not so free: that is part of what the $50 was for, but the person who took it from me did not say so), I pay to have fish, chips and tea in the restaurant. I ask for black tea but get rooibos. I say I will drink it and have what I wanted afterwards, but in the event, a search established that the only other kinds of tea available are ones I like even less.

Going back into the lounge I find it is now completely full: every lounger, settee and pouffe occupied by people and their luggage, taking up as much room as possible. Various sticky spillages and crumbs decorate the floor and furniture. I take possession of a few square inches of pouffe facing away from the television and watch one particular man. He is in his shirtsleeves, plump with soft, unmuscular fat, with a florid face and a lot of attitude. He is walking around more than necessary, with a 'look at me' gait, and a coloured silk handkerchief poking out of his back trouser pocket. All but one of the occupants are male: some are fleshy Americans, and most exude that special assured demeanour of white men accustomed to getting their own way in Africa. Noisy, domineering, repulsive. All are sticking like limpets to the most desirable chairs and power sockets. Some manly football programme is on all the screens. I ignore it, and as exhaustion begins to hit, reflect on what I most want to retain and savour of the last 48 hours. The physical setting with its dramatic lagoons; the street scene: real life, here and now; and Folawe, the bright future.

Chapter Eleven

Taipei: History and Art

Taiwan is not recognised as a country by the UK and most other governments, so there are no consular facilities, which at least obviates the need for any kind of visa. I have been invited to give two conference presentations, offering the opportunity to see a new place. Since getting back from Lagos, I have had two days at home and am booked on an evening flight to Taipei, via Bangkok, on Tuesday 5 November. So the easiest arrangement is to leave home after an early lunch, take the train to Kings Cross and the tube to Heathrow, and to hope that there are no major disruptions. Fortunately, everything goes smoothly.

Coarse young men seem to be more evident than usual at Terminal 3. When I use a toilet cubicle prior to check-in, someone nearby is making loud, vulgar suggestions as to what others, presumably his companions, are getting up to in the cubicles. Later, in departures, during my next toilet cubicle experience, a voice from next door shouts, I am not sure to whom, 'Aw! The crack of my arse is so sweaty my boxers are wet!' Cultures are on display to each other at Terminal 3. I am not proud of my countrymen. I go to the café called Rhubarb to sample their evening fare and enjoy Fentiman's dandelion and burdock, Lapsang Souchong, and oat-crunch fried chicken with chips.

I am booked into 'Elite', Eva Airways' equivalent of premium economy, so I get to use an 'Elite only' toilet which has fresh flowers.

During the boarding period, the seat-back screen is showing a programme about S E Asian birds, which is better than the usual offerings. Eva offers good service in a nice friendly manner. After arriving I learn that they are one of two Taiwanese airlines. They give out 550 ml bottles of water, then fruit juice a couple of times. 'Plum liqueur' turns out to be a light plum wine, served with ice, that tastes of stewed plums. For breakfast, not fancying the 'Western Style', I pick 'Chinese Style' and am rewarded with an enjoyable congee (rice 'porridge') with fish, peas and ginger matchsticks. On planes, I have developed a napkin routine that others probably find comical, born of my fear of ruining my only business outfit. I put the napkin provided, which is usually small, on my lap in the usual way. From my pocket, I extract a larger one and use it in the traditional manner, tucked into my shirt collar. This is a wise precaution before tackling the gloopy congee, as otherwise I would have met my hosts looking a bit of a mess.

At Bangkok, where I land mid-afternoon on Wednesday, the passengers continuing on the same plane to Taipei have to disembark. At the gate, a group of young women in uniform are chanting an explanation about something, waving plastic cards, and, typically, they all clam up as soon as they see me coming, so I have to ask, and am told the transit arrangements. These involve a long walk, in a certain direction, through security, up a level, and another long walk in the opposite direction back to the same gate. I wait to get back on the plane among a group of 13 Taiwanese stewardesses. While sitting among them, I feel that Bangkok is quite warm for my three-piece Harris Tweed suit.

At Taipei, there is much wearing of face masks. Immigrants have to walk past a fever-detecting machine, and I see its masked operatives looking suspiciously at my glowing pink head. The immigration officer is friendly and welcoming, but keeps looking at me very hard, then back at the passport, and makes a comment with a jabbing fingers motion in which I think he is saying I have staring eyes. Outside, there are crowds of people meeting arrivals, stretching in both directions: I try turning right and am relieved to see a board with 'Dandy Hotel' and my name underneath. The driver speaks no English. He takes me outside and points to a spot where I am to wait. I assume he is going to get the car.

I wait a while. All the cars seem very large, and many are of the Lexus and Mercedes category. I wonder what I will do if the driver never comes back, also whether I am supposed to be able to recognise him at a distance when he does.

Eventually the driver returns, with a mere Nissan but of truly limousine proportions. As soon as I am inside, the driver insists through gestures that I wear the seat belt and fasten it properly. This is a first in all my foreign travel. I wonder if there is a law that is enforced or whether the car would make unpleasant bleeping noises if I don't. The next day, in taxis, I notice a sign in English saying, 'buckle up or pay up', so it is the former. Both this car and the taxis, in the Asian style, have the surface between the steering wheel and the windscreen furnished with deep-pile carpet. One day I will ask why. The ride from the airport takes about 45 minutes, and in the dark, it appears to go through a nondescript landscape of motorway and mixed development. Then I notice we are in a place more like a city centre, with an older, official-looking building and a stand of neat, urban trees. Shortly after, the driver swooshes the car down an unattractive side street, into one even smaller, and then into the mouth of the hotel's parking dungeon. I have arrived. Reception know about me, give me keys, tell me about breakfast, and leave me to find my way.

The hotel expresses modernity and funkiness, but will this be of the 'boutique' variety, or the 'made in Taiwan' variety? In the room, I struggle to locate light switches and produce a dim glow which includes a fancy backlit perforated headboard. In the bathroom, I am surprised to find an ultra-tech Panasonic combined toilet and bidet with a complicated electronic control pad. Before I realise what it is, I think that it is specialised equipment for someone with complex disabilities. There are buttons for massage, power wash, spray volume control, temperature control and other functions. There are pictorial buttons. One is a bottom-shaped curve for 'rear wash'. The other looks for all the world like a human face encased in a female hair style with flip-up ends. Surely people don't put their heads down there? I discover that this symbol, which is some sort of plan of the pan, means 'front wash'. These refinements are wasted on my urgent need to relieve myself.

I am delighted to find a kettle in the room, even though it comes only with two bags of green tea. I find a black teabag in my luggage, by chance rather than design. It is about 12.30 am by the time I am ready to sleep. I can't find out how to switch off some of the lights. There are no switches near the bed, nor any switches at all for certain of the lights, which at this stage of my day is irritating. I should have guessed: eventually I find a piece of equipment like an iPad, covered in things to press. I learn how to make the room much lighter and then how to switch everything off. I wonder how, in the pitch dark, you know where to press your finger to get some light and lay worrying about that for a while. I get up to check it out, and, of course, as soon as you touch it, it glows and the problem is solved.

On Thursday morning, I enjoy a much-needed proper hot bath. It takes ages to get the water up to four inches, and I remembered with anxiety my attempt to have a bath in Beijing which resulted in a flood. That does not happen this time. I go to find breakfast, and this confirms my suspicion: this is a bed-and-breakfast hotel. Few staff, help yourself, no lunch, afternoon tea, dinner or room service. Just grab and go, and make your own arrangements for the rest of the day. The trouble is that I am short of arrangements. I have nothing planned from lunch onwards, no local currency, no knowledge of the city, no Chinese language, and no particular desire to wander about on my own. As the day progresses, I better understand this casual approach. I discover that Taipei is a much smaller city than I had imagined, laid out clearly in a grid pattern, and that it is completely safe to walk around. The event venue is actually within walking distance of the hotel.

My first contact is with Ms Chen, who kindly escorts me from the hotel to the venue, where she will also be my interpreter. She takes me walking along a main thoroughfare, Xinyi Road, opposite the Daan Forest Park, which is the view from my bedroom window. At dawn, I had seen people exercising themselves and walking around with the exaggerated arm movements that are part of the East Asian keep-fit routine. Chen leads me across major, but very orderly thoroughfares at the Xinyi-Xing Sheng intersection, to where she can hail a taxi. Swarms of scooter riders pass. The taxi takes us up Xing Sheng South Road, then right into He Ping East Road, to the venue, which is one of the host university's campuses. There, I am introduced to people, and exchange business cards in the both-hands-and-bow Chinese fashion, locate the washroom, procure tea, and check out the speaking and projecting arrangements.

In the hall are about 80 people sitting in table groups. After the opening formalities, I give my lecture, with Chen standing nearby translating line by line. This works well, although I thoughtlessly give her some hard words. After a tea break, I am part of a panel, fielding questions which are all interesting, intelligent and appreciative. Lunch is a hot, or rather, warm-ish meal in a cardboard box. Assuming I will miss out on an evening meal, I tuck in despite the impracticality of chopsticks. Surely, even thousands of years of practice does not make them a sensible implement for tackling a battered pork chop with bone in, some slobbery thing which is a kind of fish, and a pile of grains of red rice? At least the Chinese leaves, kale stems, funny mushroom slices, and dried fish mixture are possible to pick up reasonably elegantly, but my fingers ache with the effort.

After lunch, a very nice gentleman called Tzu-Bin, an academic at the university, offers, or has been detailed, to help me to enjoy Taipei. The following day I am due to receive a modest sum in local currency, and he arranges for me to collect this from the administration office a day early so that I will be solvent. After that, he will take me to the Chiang Kai Sheck (CKS) Memorial Hall.

On the way to the administration office, one of his female colleagues says something, pointing to my tie. I ask if I have spilt something on it, but no, she wants to say it is a nice smart tie. 'And you are veeeery handsome!' she adds. I return the compliment. One of the benefits of working cross-culturally is the different perceptions people have about what is attractive. It works in my favour to be among people who think that bulbous-headed goldfish are beautiful. Probably this applies in both directions. Perhaps the young women that to me look like adorable Siamese kittens are unremarkable locally.

While we are in the office, the head of department wants to see me. I am brought black tea, and this charming, fluent woman begins a conversation which flows and flows. She begins with the General Teaching Council of Scotland, and passes on to the joint writing of history textbooks by groups representing opposing sides in former conflicts. I ask her frankly about relations between Taiwan and mainland China, and learn a lot about history, culture, and contemporary politics.

When I think I should trespass no further on her time, Tzu-Bin offers me the option, which I choose, of sampling the metro rather than taking a taxi. We walk east along He Ping East Road, past the university's main campus, to the metro station. He buys me (it needs the right coin) a blue plastic disk. This is touched on a panel to enter, and then put in a slot to exit. The metro is very cheap and extremely orderly. The queues for each door of the train are marked out in painted lines, and everyone follows the rules, without this needing enforcement.

After one stop, he leads me to the CKS Memorial Hall. This must-see site includes the national theatre, concert hall and library, all built in modern times, replicating the ornate style of traditional Chinese royal palaces. There is also the Liberty Square and formal geometric gardens, which together create a vista to the memorial. This great structure, up enough steps to wear me out, contains an open-fronted chamber in which an effigy of CKS seated in state is guarded by white-uniformed soldiers. On the way, Tzu-Bin explains that many visitors from China and Japan come to the memorial, especially Chinese who do not like communism. He can identify them easily by their accents, and as we walk along he identifies one group after another as Chinese: in fact, the majority of the crowd.

We are just in time for the twice-daily changing of the guard. It is interesting how these displays of prolonged military ballet vary between countries. Here, many of their movements are in very slow motion, with moments of frozen tableau, which give quite a good dramatic effect. Faster moves include fists shot out horizontally to the front, with knees raised, which remind me, I am ashamed to say, of Malcolm McDowell in the title role of the film *Caligula*, being forced by Tiberius to do his 'Little Boots' dance. The guards take absolutely forever to present arms. Will they ever stop juggling with their bayoneted rifles? Perhaps they spin this out as long as possible because the guards coming on duty will have to stand still for eight hours. Tzu-Bin leads me down to the exhibition hall under the memorial. This is surprisingly enormous, bringing out the scale of the memorial above. Near the entrance are some craft shops, where I look at, but resist, coral and jade. In the museum, my education about CKS and Taiwan continue. It is more informative and interesting than I had expected. For example, I had not known that CKS had become a Christian in adult life: the displays include his Bible, prayers, and an Easter address. The displays also include many photographs, books and papers, military artefacts and two vintage Cadillac limousines. An educational display celebrates CKS's extension of schooling. The exhibition ends with a reconstruction of the presidential office with a waxwork of the leader of the nation. Some of the displays remind me of the exhibition at Chartwell of Churchill's life. What makes me think of this is that Tzu-Bin delights in pointing out to me photographs of CKS with Churchill and Prince Philip.

Outside, we move towards a taxi rank. A flock of sparrows, the same the world over, burst out of a tree and peck about on an expanse of lawn. Back at the Dandy Hotel, I sup on a few mini-oatcakes left over from my train ride south on Tuesday, a biscuit from the otherwise empty minibar, and two mugs of tea.

On Friday morning, hungry and eager, I go to the basement for breakfast like a confident regular. Unlike yesterday, the 'wait to be seated' sign is being acted upon. A waitress decides for me which of the many empty tables I should sit at, and removes a plastic egg-shaped object from it. I wonder what it is for: it looks like an air freshener or gnat killer, but I have not got around to sniffing it. No, it simply means that the table is free.

The delights of breakfast include Lipton's Yellow Label tea, rice soup with no added flavouring, and the daily special, which looks like a mixture of leftovers with the addition of eggs hard-boiled for a long time in a spicy mixture that colours them. A waitress of delicate, orchid-petal East Asian beauty floats to my table and prettily asks permission to take my plate. She smiles, I smile, we smile.

In the foyer, two students are gathering up the international contributors to the conference, who are all lodged in the same hotel. We are taken in a couple of taxis to the same venue, but to a different part of it. The day begins in a lecture theatre of the size and layout of a municipal council chamber. It is not a great gathering: about 120 people are present. They are academics, and it is considered acceptable to conduct the proceedings in English. High-ranking dignitaries make opening speeches. After these formalities, many of the older, and presumably more senior, of the audience depart, leaving a group of perhaps 80, mainly young, and, I assume, either postgraduate students or junior faculty. Then I am first on. I enunciate my lecture slowly and clearly, as far as possible simply reading words that the audience have in front of them on the PowerPoint slides. This may not make for very exciting entertainment, but I have found it is the most practical approach with an audience whose first language is not English. There are a few questions of clarification regarding the English educational scene, and my time slot expired. I try hard not to overrun into another presenter's time, even if the chair would allow.

After tea break, I attend an English-medium symposium with contributors from Singapore, Hong Kong, Taiwan and mainland China, whose inputs are close enough to my interests to move me to take a few notes, which is rare. One of the students who had collected us that morning, a man called Shong, is deputed to be my escort. It has been planned that I should see the National Palace Museum, and I am offered the choice for lunch of another warm picnic box, or getting something at the museum. I opt for the latter.

It is a bright sunny day, and the museum seems to be at the edge of the city, backed by densely wooded mountains. The taxi ride takes in a selection of urban scenes, and the greener areas remind me of Singapore. The museum is housed in a splendid building in the style of a Chinese palace, in a high position up many steps. Shong buys tickets and takes me to a restaurant on the top floor with spectacular views of the mountains. It is a busy dim-sum and tea house. I choose a meal selection in which everything is flavoured with pouchong tea. There are pork balls in a watery, refreshing, soup, with bits of tea leaf in them. A ball of rice steamed wrapped up in a banana leaf is rather more evidently laced with tea leaves. Dessert is a tea jelly: interesting, not sweetened, with a clean, refreshing taste, pretty much as unflavoured iced tea would taste. I also have a hot pouchong, unfortunately green rather than black. Shong chooses an iced tea and orders some dim-sum to share.

As Tzu-Bin had warned me, the museum is crowded. It is the Taiwanese equivalent of the British Museum and very similar in format and content. I am not a great one for spending hours in hot, crowded museums. A quick impression satisfies me. I feel duty-bound to show it some respect and take an interest, so I select a number of galleries and try not to rush too much. There are, of course, some fine old ceramics (how do they stay so fresh and bright for so many centuries?), and I am interested in the number of highly ornate English seventeenth-century clocks, obviously made especially for the oriental market. We decide to queue up to see one of the museum's main attractions: a Chinese cabbage carved out of jadeite, white where it should be white, and green where it should be green. I am glad I have seen it for real, but I feel no urge to go again.

I am glad to get outside, into fresh air and away from crowds. The sun is glaring on the brilliant white walls and decorative trimmings of the museum, reminding me of wedding cake icing. The mountains are covered in dense, dark, viridian green trees, sharp-edged against a metallic blue sky. In front of the museum, at a lower level, is a Chinese Garden. Our tickets let us through the turnstile and into a series of covered walkways, pagodas and water features progressing downhill. There are 'Chinese' gardens in other countries, and ambling across this willow-pattern plate, I have to remind myself that this is the real thing. The wooden structures are massively constructed, with geometric lattices, ornately carved edges, and roofs covered with large stems of bamboo, or something similar, formed into concave surfaces. The interiors of the open-sided walkways and pagodas are cool and contemplative. Some of the narrower water features are crossed by bridges of the classic semi-circular profile. A white-painted zig-zag walkway bridges a large pond teeming with enormous koi. I watch them for as long as I think reasonable to Shong, taking snapshots that I know from experience will not be very successful. Koi move too quickly: I see a nice frame-full of fish, and by the time the shutter has worked, get a picture of a few splashy tails. Various waterfowl stand lazily on a netted-off area of bank: a Taipei equivalent to St James's Park. Through the exit gate, Shong finds a taxi and takes me back to the Dandy Hotel, where I have about an hour and a half before being collected again to go to the conference banquet.

This is a pleasant occasion: a gathering for the benefit of the international visitors, who make up just under half of the 20 people present, the others being the university dignitaries hosting the event. The party is divided equally between two round tables. It is more relaxed and less socially demanding than similar events I have attended in mainland China. The Taiwanese wander around in small groups toasting each other and the visitors without putting the visitors under pressure to perform. The 'white wine' spirit is of superior aroma, flavour and smoothness to that I have experienced in Guangdong. Everyone, not just westerners, is provided with a knife and fork as well as chopsticks.

I like to drink hot tea hot, and one of the downsides at these banquets is the custom that as soon as one's teacup is emptied, it is refilled. This means that unless you want to spend the whole meal drinking endless gallons of tea, before each cup of hot tea it is necessary to drink a cold one. Early courses include small fish which taste like whitebait, in two different mixtures, one of which is hot with chilli. A later course is a big bowl of sea slugs. There are two kinds of material in this. One is slobbery, glutinous lumps of irregular shape. The other is strips; one surface of which is textured like the tread of a rubber tyre. I supposed this is the outside surface of the creature, or something it walks upon. To tackle this, I take a strip and, using a spare plate and my knife and fork, carve it into manageable pieces. I am amazed that, despite death, cooking and chopping up, the animal retains a high degree of elastic tension. I firmly impale a piece on my fork, then, halfway towards my mouth, boing! Off it flies under its own power, and I have to retrieve it from my lap or the tablecloth.

Another course looks like a chicken drumstick, but turns out to be a cleverly carved pork rib. At the dessert stage of the meal, served at the same time are a sweet pancake and a spherical object covered with small pink lumps like a grenade (the lumps, not the colour). I assume the ball will be sweet. It is a chilled and very fatty pork meatball. The final course is a jelly, pleasantly rose flavoured, but not set solid in the Western style. Gelatinous lumps of different shapes and sizes float in syrup.

On Saturday morning, I have an early drive to the airport. In daylight, I see that long stretches of this are through a green and mountainous landscape. Various carriageways glide through narrow valleys on their own separate flyovers, curving towards each other, then swinging apart. I feel as if I have been miniaturised and am going through the landscape on a model railway layout. At the airport, I change my local currency, having no prospect of returning any time soon, and am delighted to get a nice bright red £50 note. I do a quick double-take before remembering what it is, so rarely do I ever get one in England.

Chapter Twelve

Accra: Hope by the Seaside

After Taiwan, I get two weeks of normal weekly commuting before the next assignment, which I am doing with Joyce. For a while, we have been talking with Grant, an enthusiastic and amiable teacher in a middle leadership position in a London school who is keen to involve us in setting up some professional development in Ghana, which is his home country. We have had the usual debates about affordability and how to move on from the 'colonial' model of 'visiting experts', which we think is increasingly outdated, but Grant wants something high profile to set the process off, and we are keen to support him. He is putting his energy into an optimistic vision of change and shouldering the risk; we do all we can to keep our costs as low as possible.

I have been staying at the Tavistock Hotel as usual, and I spend the early part of Friday morning in the office, where I need to order some theatre tickets (the online box office only opened today) and leave my winter clothes and unnecessary luggage. Then I catch the Piccadilly line to Heathrow Terminal 5. There, I have just finished an early lunch in Gordon Ramsay's when Joyce phones to say she has arrived. We meet outside Huxley's and then she wants lunch in Gordon Ramsay's, so I have no polite alternative to going back there, giving the receptionist a double-take, and drinking a very well-constructed Bloody Mary (which contains grated celeriac) while Joyce lunches.

Grant has booked us to fly with British Airways, and the experience confirms my belief that their chosen cabin crew house-style is officiousness. No glamour, fluttering eyelashes or soft welcomes here! Staff shout and stomp around. One of them, a bald man with Royal Navy style 'full-set' whiskers takes a delight in threatening people with 'This plane isn't going anywhere until you ...' In one case, this involves, reasonably enough, removing a bin-liner sized bag of chocolate bars from someone's lap. On another occasion, after the plane has already started taxiing, this threat is directed loudly to a little girl sitting on her mother's lap, probably because she is frightened: 'This plane's going nowhere until she's sitting properly!' The child screams, believing that her actions will cause the take-off to be aborted. Sobbing, she complies. I would like to see the words in the thought balloon coming from the mother's head.

We land at Accra at 8.20 pm, and after landing, it takes half an hour for the plane to arrive at its mooring. Then it takes an hour to get through customs. The queue is in the usual zig-zag arrangement, edging forward, but often people are pushing past at normal walking speed, which no-one minds, so they must have a reason. Some come the other way. Perhaps they have not filled in the correct forms and have to go back to get them. Notices declare that all immigrants must have a valid Yellow Fever vaccination certificate, but no-one is asked to show one. Electronic fingerprinting of both hands takes place. Numerous countries now, but not the UK, can track me down if I touch things I shouldn't. Our host, Grant, meets us warmly and takes us out of the terminal to the entrance to the car park, where we wait for about another half hour for the driver to bring the car. It is dark now; both Joyce and Grant want to take photographs of us in each combination. I am pleased with how my flash-lit blue suit and buff waistcoat look in them.

Eventually, we set off for the hotel in a stout four-wheel drive vehicle. This is the usual complete mystery tour, but first, Grant helpfully takes us to his office, which is in a complex quite near to the airport, so that we can see that his organisation really exists. I am impressed: it is a reasonable facility given the embryonic stage of his project, and he seems to have a willing group of assistants, including Richard, who is acting as driver. As well as his education projects, Grant is a religious pastor, and his team are part of his flock. After quite a drive, on increasingly rutted roads, we get to the N'Joy Hotel. It looks as if everyone has gone to bed. Grant supervises check-in. No refreshment seems to be on offer, but we are presented with a form to fill in for breakfast. This offers a depressingly limited range, with the common misunderstanding about things that go together in English cuisine. If you choose bread, you can have with it *either* butter, *or* jam, *or* honey, but you cannot have butter *with* either jam or honey. After we have filled it all in, the receptionist remembers that tomorrow is Saturday and there will be a buffet.

We are shown to our rooms, and by now it is becoming clear that Grant has economised on hotel accommodation. It takes a while to organise bottled water and some hot water for making tea. Joyce, who is more assertive than me, perseveres with insisting on some toast. By the time the water has arrived, I have discovered that most of the power sockets and switches are faulty. Also, I am not surprised to find that my mobile phone does not work at all. I spill most of the hot water trying to find out how the flask opens, turning a prettily covered table into a sodden mess. An insect runs off, indignant at this disturbance. Sometime later, I am delighted when a small portion of toast and butter arrives, but without anything with which to spread the butter. One manages. The good news is getting the wireless internet working, so I can send a brief e-mail home. Then, it being 11.30 pm with a long and demanding day tomorrow, I go to bed.

Saturday morning finds me sitting on a chair drawn up to the (empty, non-functioning) fridge, on which my laptop perches, as the power socket for it is the only one functioning properly. The room is on the first floor, looking out to the front over the hotel porch and the tops of palm trees in the small, partly brick-paved front yard. Next is the road: people have been driving on the right here since 1974 to fit in with surrounding countries, most of which have French influence. Beyond the road is a stretch of bare scrubby earth and a rough earth track.

The hot water I had spilt the previous evening has incapacitated the bug which ran away from the flask, so this morning I am able to identify it as a small cockroach. The wet tablecloth has dried out completely. I spend a long time waiting to see if any hot water will come through, and remembering a lesson learnt in Yemen, climb up to investigate the controls and electrics of a water heater. Making no progress, I struggle with a puny trickle of unheated shower water (not icy cold because of the ambient temperature on the pipes), feeling very aggrieved about it. Then, when dry and dressed, I discover a switch some yards away, which makes the water heater work. What a difference a switch makes! Hot water will be something to look forward to tonight.

I meet Joyce, whose room is next to mine, and we go down to explore the breakfast buffet. This offers small, lukewarm omelettes, tiny portions of cold baked beans, bread and butter. I am delighted to see also some fried potatoes and take quite a few, but they have a weird gone-off taste like potatoes that have been left in the soil too long.

We are collected in the 4X4, which bumps its way over poor roads. I enjoy the views. We head west, so the sea is to the left, beyond shacks and scrub. Richard speeds up as we get onto a better road surface. We pass a military academy training school. The sea is blue, the sky is blue, and the soil is red, because this is Africa. The vegetation is brown and green, and crisp, clear light shines through the leaves and branches in a particularly African way. Where a stream joins the sea at an inlet, I get a brief glimpse of foaming breakers. On the right, plants are growing up canes on an allotment-style patch. Some small fishing boats are visible in the distance. We pass a construction site and a very bumpy stretch of road. In front, two men are riding on a swaying lorry steadying piles of goods in polythene bundles. A roadside awning on a rough patch of ground covers fancy bedroom furniture for sale: a surreal combination of mock Louis XIV styling and dry tussocks. There are chickens in a roadside coop, and market stalls on every available patch of ground. We try to swat the mosquitoes flying around inside the car: I do not bother with anti-malaria tablets on short trips because of their side effects. The earth is turning less red, to a hue more like the colour of light tan shoe polish. There is a mixture of new commercial buildings, and piles of stone blocks - for sale or use?

Turning into sideroads, we pass through an area where fancy houses and crude shacks form a congested mixture. Rolled barbed wire on the top of walls is quite common. Ditches run alongside roads and across wasteground. Some are dry; some have standing, unpleasant-looking water of the kind that mosquitoes love. We cross a dusty, single-track railway running through a densely populated area with no protective fencing. Richard said that fatal accidents were very rare. It is apparent that the people are religious. Pentecostal churches and temples abound, notices advertise bible classes, and many shops carry overtly religious slogans. Richard drives very slowly indeed over road humps, of the style I had first noticed in Yemen, sufficiently kerb-like to be treated with respect. The side roads are of red earth, bounded by dense shacks and market stalls stretching back some distance.

Back on a more major road, there are delicate, acacia-like trees, and bushes carry bright cerise and pink blossoms, and women carry watermelon slices and other produce on their heads with haughty elegance. Many small roadside kiosks sell a range of products including green coconuts cut for drinking. Some of the kiosks have shacks behind them that could be living quarters. We pass a Guinness distribution depot opposite a family health hospital. A man is carrying an old sewing machine on his shoulder, supported on an olive-green cushion. It is like a Singer: black with gold tracery.

Nearing our destination, we see on the left the Freedom and Justice Arch in Independence Square, with its seating terraces around a plaza; buildings of government ministries, a tall building with Movenpick in red neon letters, so presumably an upmarket hotel; tower blocks under construction, and a large tree dangling a crop of bean pods. The journey has taken about 45 minutes. Our venue, in central Accra near the National Theatre, is the British Council headquarters: a category of building which has a certain architectural sameness, in the manner of British prisons.

The event has been well-prepared. A team of students (this is Saturday) act as greeters, giving out bits and pieces to delegates (it emerges later that the main pack of materials for delegates has not come back from the printers in time). The teaching room is a tall, airy hall, with a raised stage (not used until the evening event), large screens, and seating mainly in theatre style, which enables numbers to be packed in but limits the scope for organising group discussions.

Our activity was originally designed as a two-day school leadership programme. To cut costs to match expected income, Grant has reduced the duration to a single day (which of course we know about), but has also widened the range of people enrolled, with the effect that we become gradually aware that the focus of our material does not match the interests of some delegates.

The venue would be ideal for religious worship, and Grant starts off the day with some warm-up interactions which create something of the same celebratory fellow-feeling and expectancy. We do the business. Joyce and I take turns to perform: I am not sure to what effect, but the evaluations are reasonable. A savoury biscuit and a bottle of water are issued to each delegate mid-morning. A late lunch of tasty Jollof rice is served picnic-style in the garden. In the box with the rice come a piece of chicken, a sort of cabbage leaf and a small pot of very hot fish sauce. Because I have to avoid drinks containing citrus fruit, bottled water is my drink for the day. The lunch is pleasant and everyone is friendly.

We give more presentations. Grant is keen that our programme should end at about 4.00 pm to allow time for preparations for the evening event. Joyce and I have to hang about in a steamy room with no refreshment until 5.45 pm for the ceremony. During that period, we study the evaluation forms. Near the end of this time, one of the student helpers offers to go and get us some tea from a hotel, but we feel that would take too long to fit in before the start of the event. It is difficult to believe that a British Council national headquarters campus contains no source of tea: perhaps it would be different on a weekday.

The evening ceremony is the official launch of Grant's educational enterprise. It is planned that I will make one of the speeches as senior representative of our organisation. No slot had been planned for Joyce, but as we are ushered to our front-row seats, Grant says, 'You have a slot, Joyce'. The audience seems to include some significant dignitaries as well as Grant's family, friends and religious community. The high stage is used. Overall, the event seems like a memorial service at which speaker after speaker eulogises the deceased, except that Grant is very much alive, standing spot-lit while a compere directs proceedings. Films play on the screens, in which Grant does not appear, but educators he has worked with in East London expound on his qualities and the changes he has wrought in their lives and professional experiences. Some of the speakers are clergymen who, with thankful praise, identify the spiritual significance of the proposed developments.

Then, with an elaborately respectful introduction, Joyce is cued to the platform. Considering that she has nothing pre-prepared, her speech is fluent, appropriate to the occasion, of good length and commendable in every way. The only issue from my point of view is that it covers everything I might have said. The applause subsides and it is my turn. Three years ago, I would have been panic-stricken into embarrassed awkwardness. I mount the stage with what I hope looks like assurance while my mind races. I adopt a ponderous, majestic style of speaking to give myself thinking time. I introduce myself at some length and explain my work, saying that this is my 47th international liaison on behalf of my organisation. That gets applause – it is a friendly audience. I describe how the thinking behind our international work has changed since the colonial era; how many approaches we receive from people wanting to be partners get rejected; how we met Grant; what a great guy he is; and what we plan for the future. It is enough. Then, as pre-arranged, I present Grant with a framed certificate, impressive-looking but in fact a mock-up, purporting to be a treaty between our organisations, which Grant has caused to be made, purely for the purposes of this photo opportunity. Thus, with much prayer and blessing, Grant's enterprise is launched.

Inevitably, given the nature of the occasion, Grant needs to interact with well-wishers and distinguished guests, so there is another long period with nothing to do. While we are waiting for Grant, a very well-dressed man introduces himself as Michael, and starts a conversation about Ghana's oil resources, which he considers have been developed on terms over-generous to the oil companies. He discusses Chinese investment, including their policy of offering attractive short-term aid and investment packages in return for long-term rights over minerals and other natural resources, and Western foreign policies. This helps to pass the waiting time very pleasantly. It then transpires that Michael is joining us for dinner.

Heavy rain has been falling. It stops conveniently just as Grant joins us and we set off, with Richard driving, following the coast eastwards. On the way, Michael explains that he had grown up in the area, pointing in the dark down the relevant side street. I take the opportunity to ask a question that has puzzled me about developing country townscapes generally, including here. How does land ownership work in these areas of higgledy-piggledy development where all sorts of shacks and kiosks occupy odd bits of seemingly waste ground? Michael explains that in Ghana most of the land is owned by families rather than by individuals, and usually the in-fill small enterprises are run by people connected to the family. Occasionally, where that is not the case, rent is paid to the family. He says that where big new developments are taking place, the investors have to negotiate the purchase of the land from the family.

Grant directs Richard to park at La Palm Royal Beach Hotel, telling us it is the poshest venue around. Inside, the foyer is full of extremely glamorous, made-up, very fragrant young women, wearing tight miniskirts at the micro-pelmet end of the spectrum. They are nice to be near, but I wonder what they are doing. Later, on the way out, I see the answer on the events board: 'Miss Nigeria in Ghana finals'.

After a brief survey of the eating options inside ('Continental' means southern Europe: is not Africa a continent?) Grant leads us into the garden between the hotel and the sea, where we walk on wet paths past various wet shrubberies to an open-air restaurant under a roof in the style of traditional huts, called Ghanaian Village, which specialises in local cuisine. Had it not been dark, there would be a good view of the sea. Hardly anyone else is here. The staff find us chairs that are not too wet; the table is rain-spattered, and our feet are in puddles. We had walked past the cooking area on the way in to get an idea of what might be on offer. When the waitress comes, I choose a grilled seafood platter as a simple, safe choice because it is bound to be good. Grant orders something with something else, either a side dish or starter, and the waitress tells him he can't: 'No, you can't have that – that would be too rich and filling, you would have indigestion!' Grant is nonplussed: he is used to being obeyed, especially when choosing dishes in restaurants, and he argues his case to be allowed to give more custom, but in the end he acquiesces. When the food comes, the portions do indeed look enormous, but that is partly because of the thick tiles on which they are served. The seafood is excellent: giant prawns and chewy slabs of squid on a bed of rice, with the usual hot fish sauce.

I had assumed the 'La' of 'La Palm' was to give a French or Spanish flavour for tourists, but Michael says it is named after the town, which is called Labadi 'because it is bad'. The Labadi Hotel is the next one along. He talks about this stretch of beach, saying there are only three places where the beach is safe for swimming, because elsewhere it is rocky and steeply shelving. Here by the hotel, there is a tollgate to the beach, and it is only used heavily on four or five occasions a year for public holiday events. Along the coast generally there are a few small kiosks: it has not been developed as a resort which he sees as a wasted opportunity. He thinks that further along the coast a Lebanese investor has bought property previously owned by an Englishman and will be doing some development. Some years ago, it had been worth next to nothing, but now a one-bedroom flat is costing $250,000. As the meal proceeds, Grant, Michael and Joyce talk in some detail about physical punishments during childhood at school and home, a topic I do not wish to join in with or prolong. I get to bed at 12.30 am, not having had time or energy to test out the hot water.

On Sunday morning, our hosts are in church, so the plan is that Joyce and I will breakfast separately, work in our own rooms, then meet up a bit before lunch. The breakfast is the same as the buffet version but smaller and slower. I do some e-mailing, but power cuts mean that I am sitting in a funny posture in front of the fridge to little advantage. Joyce, being far in advance of me in ownership and use of electronic gadgetry, has checked in online for the flight home, and urges me to do the same. This depends on the hotel being able to print my boarding card from a forwarded e-mail attachment, assuming I succeed in reaching that stage. The receptionist is willing, and gives me the hotel's e-mail address. I manage, impressing myself. The boarding pass arrives to my normal work e-mail account, and I forward it to the hotel. The system rejects the address. I go to reception and they suggest a slightly different version of the address. That is rejected also; they suggest a further variation, with the same result, whereupon I decide to check-in at the airport. A short while later, one of the previous attempts does, somehow, get through, and with close supervision and a lot of help from colleagues, the receptionist is able to print the boarding pass. The only previous time I have got a hotel to do this was at the Black Swan in Helmsley where it was more straightforward. I think it might help the hotel's business if the staff know its e-mail address.

For lunch, I choose a starter of fried plantains, followed by fish and chips: a plain option because I am worried about the state of my stomach and the long period of time there will be between leaving the hotel and reaching airport facilities. Joyce chooses a soup and a substantial fish dish. To drink, and needing to avoid citrus fruit, I ask if they have ginger ale. No, but they make a ginger juice. I ask about it. 'Well, we just juice the ginger and add a bit of sugar.' Bravely, I go for it. A big glass of opaque buff fluid arrives. The first sip makes my eyes water. It is powerful magic, cruelly refreshing. The last sip makes me feel I have achieved something. During the meal, I spot an enormous lizard, definitely into dragon category, making its leisurely, wiggle-hipped way up a sloping drive outside. Also during the meal, Richard bounds in, dressed flamboyantly to the nines in his Sunday best. He draws a chair up to the side of our table, which is of a size to accommodate only two people, and orders food. He is thoroughly churched-up, glowing with zeal.

Grant arrives, and with smooth efficiency checks us out, settles bills, and says we will do some sightseeing on the way to the airport. There had previously been some worrying mention of shopping malls, the last thing I would want to traipse around, but in the event Grant's taste and judgement prove impeccable. Michael joins us: he is making a brief visit to Ghana and using the opportunity to catch up with Grant. As always, Richard is the driver.

The journey into Accra is becoming familiar, but I see fresh sights, including the Labadi Hotel, next to where we had been last night. I learn that Kofi Annan is Ghanaian, as we pass the Kofi Annan Institute

Training Centre. On the left, towards the sea, Michael points out something I would have missed. 'Keep looking, I'll show you something special', he says. I see dune-like features covered with coastal vegetation. He makes us keep looking, and then points out some poles, the significance of which I would have overlooked. They are on a ridge, in a row, and each has a square board at its top, numbered from one to eight. Below the ridge is a gully, and part way up the other side, a low concrete bunker or pill-box. 'The firing squad', Michael explains. Up until 1981, this had been in frequent use as the place where people the ruling regime didn't like were brought for execution.

Coming out of Labadi, we pass an area that used to be a vibrant fishing community, devoid of much activity now. Near here is the place where Michael lived as a child. We pass a modern bar called Gold Coast Lounge, and a shanty area developed in and around old colonial buildings. Near to the railway station, there is a vast area of market stalls, with a fuzzy boundary between road surface and market, and the smallest goats I have ever seen. A young woman is selling coconuts with amazing poise, like an elegant, slender, haughty camel. Areas are jammed full of the minibuses which provide the main form of public transport. We stop for gasoline: so far as I can remember, the first time I have seen this globally standard transaction in a developing country. A bit further on, Richard turns sharp left, and passing an incongruously located field of geese, parks in Castle Drive, near to the house ('castle') used at one time as the president's residence. It was built by the Dutch in the seventeenth century: Dutch and Portuguese influence had impacted before the British came.

We walk to Asomdwe Park (meaning 'peace'), which is the site of the mausoleum of the only President of Ghana to have died in office. His grave has pride of place, backed by a wall constructed in a striking 'V'-shaped design. A South African flag marks the recent visit of Jacob Zuma, who has laid a wreath. Leading up to this focal point is a double row of rectangular patches of gravel headed with wooden box-like features. These are the grave spaces reserved ready for the next couple of dozen presidents. Whether they will occupy these modest plots or perhaps choose something grander of their own remains to be seen. The trees are strewn with ribbons in the national flag colours, which Michael summarises as being red for the blood of struggle, yellow for the gold coast, and green for vegetation, with the black star representing human capital. There are no sentries or other forms of security for this special place.

A further short drive brings us to Independence Arch and Black Star Square, where, in 1957, Nkruma made his first speech to the newly independent nation: the first British colony to gain independence. Grant and Michael both give first-hand accounts of the annual march-past by school children on Independence Day. Grant leads us through the end of the square towards the beach, reached through a sort of toll gate. No money is required today, but on the way back, Grant chastises someone who is posing as an official, illegally collecting entry fees.

I am interested to see the beach. The backshore is of hummocky dune-like features, covered with vegetation remarkably similar to that at Spurn Point on the Yorkshire coast: undoubtedly different species, but with the same drought-resistant, low, wind-blasted, barren soil-clinging survival habits. This opens out to a panoramic view of the South Atlantic. Looking out over the incoming rollers, eyes stinging in the breeze, the next land is Antarctica. The red soil of Africa, which I can see now is in fact clay, forms low, soft cliffs, giving way to the beach itself, and clearly subject to slumping and coastal erosion. Here are further similarities to Holderness: clay, erosion, strong onshore breeze, and a lighthouse on a headland. I take in the scene, the only person for miles around wearing a business suit: when I travel light, I have no other outfit. Groups of people are running in and out of the waves, and sitting around or playing on the beach, it being Sunday afternoon. These are ordinary people, the local population at leisure. The basic facilities include a crude shack for changing in, and a stall selling kebabs and soft drinks. As Michael had said, it is undeveloped, but had it been developed, these people could not have afforded to come here.

Back in the car, we pass the grave of the unknown soldier, the Supreme Court in its classical style columns, the High Street and General Post Office - the oldest section of the town, and the Bank of Ghana. Joyce is keen to buy some genuinely local sandals, and Richard drives into a yard area of galleries and craft shops, but we decide to come back later in order to be in time to enter the Nkruma National Park.

While in this yard, I have a surprising encounter. The car is immediately accosted by a group of young men, determined to exploit us financially. With practised friendliness, they say their names, smiling and getting too close, and start offering us all kinds of 'bargains'. One young man, with braided hair, as part of his chatty routine to establish familiarity, asks me, 'You're from England, aren't you? Where in England?' The simplest answer would be to say 'London', that being my work base, but I feel inclined to be a bit awkward in the face of this onslaught, and so with literal truthfulness say, 'Barnard Castle'. To my astonishment, this apparently local lad in a back yard in Accra, with a great beam, says, 'Ah that's fantastic, it's lovely there! I'm from Newcastle, I'm the only Geordie here!'

We find a place to leave the car near one of the many entrances to the Nkruma National Park and enter this shrine to the father of the nation. My first impression is of a carefully and respectfully maintained garden of great tranquillity. Some peacocks peck around under neatly trimmed trees, all labelled with their species and origin. One has bright red blossom. Another is a Vietchia Palm, which I notice because it is similar to, but not quite the same, as one of the palm trees outside our hotel. A mango tree had been planted by Nelson Mandela.

We come to the central area where there are water features, fountains, stone walkways, steps, statues and the mausoleum. A wedding party are using it as the backdrop for their photography. Grant and Michael find this a strange, morbid choice, but I can see its visual attractions. Nkruma's Cadillac, which is in poor, unrestored condition, is displayed in a glass case. It is not labelled in any way, but later in the museum there is a picture of him in it, standing to acknowledge the crowds.

A recently sculpted statue of Nkruma stands before the mausoleum. An old one, which had its head ripped off, is further on, near to the entrance to the museum: it had been mobbed in the 1966 riots, by which time Nkruma had become very autocratic and socialist. The CIA were said to have been involved in his downfall in the coup of that year led by the police and military. The destruction of the statue by an avenging mob was similar to that following the fall of Saddam Hussein. The mausoleum is of modern design, with a series of vertical spines, each with an outward-facing point made from two concave surfaces. The overall effect makes me think of a miniature version of Coventry Cathedral. It is surrounded by water, and entered across a bridge. In the dark, cool interior, Nkruma's grave is marked with a simple flat stone slab, with 1909-1972 and other basic information. His Egyptian wife, Fathia (1932-2007), has been buried beside him.

The museum is a single room in a kind of basement bunker. It charts the key points of Nkruma's life. He had been a teacher and the General Secretary of the Gold Coast Convention. He wrote a lot of books, mainly about why the colonies should be freed. His PhD thesis is displayed, and family photographs with his first and second wives. Uniforms and other clothes, a desk, and photographs of his high points as a statesman complete the exhibition. Nkruma had been a leading figure in the West African Alliance, and when ousted from being President of Ghana, had, for a spell, been Co-President of Guinea.

Thus educated, we go back to the craft yard to look for sandals. Grant decides it is easier to walk than to try to drive. This involves picking our way along the uneven rubble at the edge of a main road, with quite a lot of people coming in the opposite direction. I feel self-conscious, but not at all unsafe. This walk in particular confirms the truth of what I had been told in Lagos, that 'Ghana is Africa for beginners'. My main impression is of very religious, law-abiding citizens, and the virtual absence of police or other security forces. Back at the yard, our previous acquaintances leap to our service. The ringleader says, 'OK follow me' and sets off away from the public area among what look like dwelling huts. I am immediately alarmed and hang back, letting Grant take charge. I am envisaging robbery, kidnap or murder. Grant calls a halt, crossly insisting we go to the shop. Later he explains that these men have an agency agreement with the shop. Their plan is to get us seated in a hut while one of them brings produce from the shop to offer us at inflated prices. They are good-natured about being rumbled and come to the shop with us. There, Grant asks to deal with the proprietor only. Joyce gets her sandals. I resist everything, including an offer from a boy outside to make me a woven bracelet with my name on it. We walk back to the car by a through-cut which means we do not have to walk along the road again. As we approach, we see a man finishing off washing the car: he says he is unemployed, and can't stand having nothing to do, so he washes cars whether or not their owners want to pay him.

We arrived at the place where the buses stop, and Michael takes his leave: a nice guy and smooth conversationalist from first to last. Richard drives us on towards the airport. The plan is that we will stop and have tea somewhere to fill in some time. On that final leg of the drive, I am seriously exhausted: three-quarters asleep but kept slightly conscious by a bursting, thumping, overheated head, and an uncomfortable bowel that is, in its different way, feeling equally overheated and bursting. We arrive at the tearoom, and only then it becomes clear that Grant knows this place and uses it often and that it is right next to the airport.

Richard has driven us everywhere we went in Accra. He is a smart and reputable young man: an employee of Grant's enterprise and a member of his church community. But the social distinction of the chauffeur remained. When we looked at sights, he would come with us, and he came to our table in the N'Joy Hotel, but when Grant had taken us to the La Palm restaurant the previous evening, and now at this more humble tearoom, he makes himself scarce.

My first port of call is the toilet, then I go in and join the table chosen by Joyce and Grant. We order tea, for which I yearn, and in the meantime, I take some Pro-Plus tablets to keep me awake. A large pot of tea arrives, which I take black as always, and it is strong enough, made with three teabags, to withstand a fair bit of sugar for energy. The others add milk, of the thick, pale brown evaporated kind, which is the standard local offer. Tea and conversation make me feel slightly more human. The pot empties, and with it being so strong, Joyce suggests getting it filled with some hot water on the same bags. The waiter doesn't seem clear about what to do: 'You want me to bring hot water' and started to take the whole tray away. Grant instructs in his authoritative way, picking up the pot and explaining, 'put the tray down, take this pot, add more hot water to it.' When it comes back, this leads to a conversation about how hot each of us drink tea, and Grant, explaining his own tendency in this matter, recounts a childhood ritual rite of passage he had endured which involved having to drink a very hot cow's blood mixture without blowing on it first. This abusive experience has made a lasting impression on him.

When it is time to make a move, Grant says it is better to walk to the drome rather than take the car. I hadn't realised it was so near, and it is an odd experience: you can't just walk into Heathrow, although I had sometimes wished it was possible as an alternative to taxi fares. Grant and Richard come in with us to help, right up to the immigration area, then take their leave. Through in departures, I drink some more tea, and pass some more burning chilli. Boarding the plane, which is a full-size Boeing 777, involves walking across the tarmac to it - a new experience with a large plane. There are ladders to the front and rear entrances. No-one is using the rear, although that has been designated for the rows Joyce and I are in, so we blazed the trail. 'Don't walk under the wing!' a man shouts, indicating we should make a wing-shaped detour around a bollard placed under the tip. After the flight gets going, British Airways offer the usual 'Fish or lamb?' challenge, repeating and shouting those two words if anyone seems unclear. I ask, 'Can you describe them a bit more than that?', and am told the fish is cod, with mashed potato and vegetables, and the lamb comes with rice and hot spices. This is quite material information given my fragile condition. I pick the fish, and have been enjoying its bland palatableness for quite a while before realising that the 'cod' is, in fact, chicken, which demonstrates how assumptions influence the senses, and how tastebuds are dulled at altitude.

Chapter Thirteen

Lahore: A Long Farewell

On Friday 7 March 2014, I set off for Lahore, for another Take Time Out conference, taking a journey from Darlington to Gatwick, which is broken by a visit to the office to leave my other passport and visa application for my next assignment, which is in Kazakhstan, and, as it turns out, for a flurry of e-mailing concerning liaison with that republic. After which I take a taxi ride to Vauxhall (the extravagance being necessary because I am running well behind time), for a pleasant and productive work session with a headhunter in the offices next to the MI5 fortress on Albert Embankment. From that office, I wheel my suitcase to Vauxhall tube station for the short ride to Victoria, where I buy a return ticket for the Gatwick Express.

I step aboard one just about to leave, and am surprised by an initial impression that it is jam-packed: standing room only. I dump my suitcase against a heap of others and move through the carriage. Then I see the problem: not that the train is full, but that so many people choose not to occupy their single seat in a polite manner. I pass bay after bay of four seats around a table, in which the two aisle seats are occupied by big noisy people with knees and elbows splayed out, and hand-luggage beside them, making it absolutely clear that they need all four seats and are not to be budged without affray.

Of course they win because moving down there is no difference between one bay and the next. No-one seems smaller or more attractive, so there is no obvious choice of whom I should confront to exercise my right to disrupt them, climb around, and trap myself in four inches of seat underneath their sweaty armpit and thigh. So I walk on by, eventually intruding myself into an airline style aisle seat beside a large but reasonably civilised gentleman (well, at least he is reading something), where I concentrate on the *Times* crossword, which I suspect of having a couple of clues which I regard as not entirely playing fair with the rules of the game: a view confirmed tomorrow when I look at the answers.

I walk through the car park to the Hilton and check in. A helpful gentleman explains that the stay is pre-paid, and they will charge any extras to the same credit card, so there is nothing for me to worry about: I can just drop my key in the box when I leave. Also, free wi-fi connection is available in bar areas only: he gives me a slip of paper with the password. In my room, whilst enjoying a welcome peppermint tea, in the gloom of inadequate lighting, I discover that the television does not work, producing only a fuzzy screen. Mindful that these facilities are costing me, I phone reception and an engineer comes. He does something to the aerial; it works; he shows me the pay for view films, and leaves it on a news channel, which is fine.

I want to bring forward the evening to offset an early start the next day, so at 5.30 pm I go down to the 'open all hours' Garden Restaurant to find it closed until 6.00 pm. I sit by the entrance and have a go with the internet access, as I want to establish contact with Eleanore. The connection seems quite slow and weak, and keeps breaking up, so I do the bare minimum. 6.00pm passes; an initial flurry of people have gone in, so I go and stand by the 'wait to be seated' sign, and after a long wait am shown to a table. I eat and sign the bill.

Back in the room, while the television might have been fixed, I find that the handset is defective. Probably the batteries are weak, but also the back is dropping off: it is physically falling to pieces. It takes 20 or 30 jabs at the screen to achieve a single interaction. When I go to the 'films' view it produces a notice saying, 'service not available', so at that point I decide to give up. I put my mobile phone on charge and top up the credit. I remember that my razor needs charging and I had not had time to do that before leaving home, so take it to the bathroom to find a shaver socket. I can't believe a modern Hilton hotel would not have a shaver socket, so I keep searching around, poking various surfaces and fittings, but in vain. What if someone is staying here for a week? Some of the fittings I poked seem about to fall off the wall. I decide to have a bath as there won't be time in the morning. It takes a long time to get a few inches of tepid water: not quite the luxurious experience I had expected. The toilet needs two or three flushes to remove evidence of moderate usage. I set three alarms for 4.45 am and get into bed.

The phone rings: it is the Garden Restaurant. They can't close my account because reception has not authorised charging extras to my room account. I express surprise, repeating what the receptionist had told me, and further explaining that I have gone to bed as I have an early start. After again explaining his own perspective in some detail, the man I am speaking with very generously says that I do not need to go downstairs and that he will speak with reception.

I wonder if I will be allowed back in the Garden Restaurant for breakfast without some kind of fuss. Serving the full breakfast range from 5.30 am is one of the (to my mind, diminishing list of) benefits of using the Hilton. I am received without challenge, which feels like crossing the border of a potentially awkward country. The food puts the Tavistock in its place: as well as being of much classier specification, the range includes black pudding, mushrooms and hash browns, all missing from the latter's workaday breakfast routine.

I do a final e-mail check in the foyer, which is worthwhile as Eleanore has responded, agreeing to meet at departures. Then I make the easy walk to South Terminal and ride the shuttle to North Terminal. Check-in is straightforward. Through into the now-familiar environment of departures, I buy a copy of the *Times* and sit for a while in Pret a Manger with porridge and tea. The departure gate is crowded, but the people there include some it is no hardship to look at or be near to. Zones are called for boarding, and I am starting to worry whether Eleanore is cutting it fine when she appears at my elbow from nowhere.

Emirates do their usual trick of leaving the 'fasten seatbelts' sign on for virtually the whole journey, and spinning out the meal service. When it does finally come, I follow the starter of dill-marinated baby shrimps and chickpea salad, by selecting as the main course slightly smoked slow-cooked beef, which is fine. Later, afternoon tea is served: a tiny finger sandwich of chicken in a lurid pink sauce, and another of cheese and pickle, which I left, and a small scone with clotted cream and strawberry jam. During the flight, Eleanore, with donnish diligence and enthusiasm, marks five essays and rehearses what she is going to be doing in Lahore, while I doze over the *Times* crossword.

At Dubai, there is time to make the connection comfortably, but not enough to have tea, only a toilet visit. I wonder about something I have noticed on previous occasions. In the men's toilets in the airport at Dubai, the water in the pans is hot: how and for what purpose I can't imagine, but it is a strange sensation, sitting over a cooking pot. I learnt the answer a few months later in Riyadh, after the period covered by this book: in some toilets, the bottom-washing hosepipe is connected to the hot tap. Eleanore is planning to meet up in the terminal for lunch with an acquaintance on our return journey – Dubai is that kind of crossroads – and I describe Oberjin, where I had enjoyed breakfasts, as a possible lunch venue, so we stop to check it out as we walk past it on the way to the gate.

Boarding the second leg of the flight involves jostling, negotiating vast volumes of other people's hand luggage, and people who find it difficult to identify and sit in their allocated seat. I am next to a man who is in the wrong seat, speaks no English, is heavily built, and smells stale, but not nearly as badly as the acridly-sweaty old man whose seat it really is, now mercifully further away. There is something of a battle for space, and in order not to cede more territory than necessary, I put up with a greater degree of hot close contact than I might have chosen. Later this man dozes off, keeling heavily in my direction. I have taken out a light novel from my hand luggage to keep me amused, which is a good choice because I am too sleepy to do anything useful, but too uncomfortable to sleep. The overhead reading lamp points unhelpfully at someone else:

when the 'fasten seatbelt' sign eventually goes off for a few seconds I stand up and make adjustments.

A member of the cabin crew, who had 'liked the colour of my suit' on boarding, and had been approving when I said I had bought it in Lahore, is now making a crouching progress along the aisle squirting two kinds of perfume into the edge of the carpet. One of her colleagues comes along behind vigorously discharging a can of air freshener. These ministrations are nothing to do with me, of course. The staff seem disorganised and start serving the meal quite late. The choice is 'chicken or lamb', and when I ask for more information am told 'they both come with rice'. 'Are they both curries?', I ask, and am told 'yes'. I pick chicken, guessing it might be milder, being wary of meals on flights into Pakistan, but in fact, it is fiery whereas the lamb, which Eleanore chose, is a biryani.

With the meal debris collected, and lights dimmed for landing, Eleanore bends over her marking, continuing to give intensely considerate and encouraging feedback to her fortunate students. Despite the stewardess's shouted commands to 'sit down', passengers behave like an unruly class being released at the end of term. Disembarkation cards are not issued on board, nor available in racks in the terminal. In the queue for 'foreign passport holders', I notice passengers off a PIA flight filling in a version marked with PIA, and wonder what the system is. Eleanore, ahead of me at the immigration counter, asks for a form and is issued a different version. When I get nearer, I ask for a form also. Seeing that we are together, the official asks if my information is the same as Eleanore's, and then excuses me from filling it in. So that is the system.

The baggage claim area is a tremendous scrum. My case comes through quite quickly. Eleanore waits ages for her case, which she describes as very bright pink. I strain my eyes, hoping to spot it, and it is surprising how many pink objects, or cases wrapped in pink film, come through. Big bottles of water come through, so it is clear that an incoming flight had a returning Umrah party. I know the sinking feeling Eleanore has of waiting so impossibly long, when a few unclaimed items keep coming around again, but also know from experience not to give up too soon, and eventually, the shocking pink case appears. The customs official excuses us from putting the cases through security: I have adopted my urgent, official look. Through the doors, a sea of faces and the smell of rose petals confirm the homecoming reception parties for returning pilgrims. Among the crush, we see the welcome sight of our names on a board and fight a passage through to the outskirts of the crowd, where an Avari Hotel official introduces us to our driver.

The first part of the drive goes smoothly enough, but we are pulled over at the same army checkpoint where I have been stopped before. A soldier, not someone senior or inspiring confidence, sticks his head in the window and asks the driver what country we are from. When we say 'England', he wants to take our passports, and the driver collects them and goes off with the soldier. We wait for what seems a very long ten minutes in an undefended car with the ignition key in, wondering what they are doing with the passports. Silly fears arise: I wonder if they are copying them, and think perhaps that if we had named some less desirable homeland such as Albania, they might not have bothered. Eventually the driver brings them back with no word of explanation, and we proceed. Later, Taymur assures us we can trust the army. The problem, he says, is that an American secret agent accidentally killed a Pakistani colleague, putting yet more strain on that already strained alliance, and they would want to know whether or not we are British secret agents.

It is good to get inside the Avari Hotel. I greet the man on reception. He produces a key card and form to sign, tells us about internet access throughout the building, and breakfast times, and offers to have tea sent up. At this apparent completion of business, Eleanore asks if she also could have a room, and the receptionist's misunderstanding is rectified.

I get to the room at 3.25 am. The suitcase arrives shortly afterwards. I wonder if the offer of tea has been acted upon or whether I should make my own, but a pot of Lipton's Yellow Label arrives at 3.50, which is most welcome. Whilst drinking it, I have a brief internet session. Music is playing, faintly but audibly: I wonder if someone is having a late party outside, and listen at the window, and then along the corridor. It seems loudest in the room, and I discover a radio has been turned on. In the bathroom, I put my razor on charge and note the very long, strong toilet flush. Thus in the space of a few minutes, the Avari demonstrates it has qualities the Hilton had not.

On Sunday morning, having gone to bed at 4.30 am and to sleep at about 5.00 am, I wake naturally at 7.30 am and decide it is better to get on with the day rather than trying to sleep any more. I go to breakfast at 8.15 am in Kim's Restaurant, choosing from the buffet a puree, some baked beans, a chicken sausage, the local version of 'hash brown' (this looks and eats like a mashed potato patty, but if you dissected the middle, you can see that it has been made from grated potato) and some pickled ginger. Tea is poured at the table: an extremely strong dark infusion the consistency of espresso coffee. A couple of fat old men are enjoying breakfast nearby. One, wearing a flowing tent of a brown Shalwar Kameez, is about four feet in diameter.

Before returning to my room, I wander around the ground floor to see whether the shops have changed since my last visit, and look through the glass doors, currently locked, to the garden. Birds are energetically enjoying the morning: pigeons, crows and sparrows, all similar to their European equivalents, and a local form of starling, perhaps the Common Myna. Later, when the shops are open and fully functioning, I look at the tailor's but find the stock range and the staff to have deteriorated.

Eleanore had said to expect her to be up sometime towards midday, but when I phone her shortly after noon she is still asleep, so after apologising for disturbing her, I go back to Kim's to eat moderately of the lunch buffet. Meanwhile an e-mail from Taymur says he will arrive in Lahore at 9.00 pm. I drift about half-asleep, waiting for a meeting scheduled for 3.00 pm with two visitors. Eleanore appears at teatime, after I had started my meeting, which I invite her to join.

Sarah had e-mailed me to ask advice about studying for a doctorate. As she is based in Lahore, I said that I was visiting soon and it would be better to meet for a discussion. She arranged for her colleague Tehmina to come with her (both are in senior management positions in a group of schools) and told me to 'look out for a woman wearing full black hijab.'

I sit in the foyer lounge in a position with a good view of the front door. They are instantly recognisable because the hijab is unusual in Pakistan. Tehmina wears the clothes of the region; Sarah is, in the style

I associate mainly with Arabia, head to foot in black, including gloves and the full face veil leaving a narrow slit for her eyes. She moves with alluring feminine grace; I bow in greeting: as I expected, she keeps her hands firmly by her sides. Tehmina's ideas and aspirations are less formulated: it is mainly Sarah's meeting. I listen and then challenge her, guiding her to take her thinking up a few gears. Apart from her CV, it is her eyes and voice only that I can build acquaintance with. In professional attitudes and interests, and in her manner of conversing with me, she presents as a sophisticated, highly educated, thoroughly modern western woman. I am interested in what this says about my own stereotyping, but had I had this conversation first, by telephone, and then met her, I would have been thrown by an apparent contradiction between her personal and professional persona, and her chosen dress persona.

We take tea. I watch Sarah drinking: holding the lower edge of her veil forward a little, and raising the cup underneath it. From time to time, she pulls up the top edge of the veil, if perhaps five millimetres of bridge of nose had become exposed, with the same movement with which a woman in western clothes might pull up an over-exposing low-cut neck-line. Because she wears gloves, I wonder what her hands are like. Towards the end of the conversation, it emerges that Sarah and Tehmina are registered to participate in the events that Eleanore and I are leading, so there will be further opportunities to talk.

Eleanore and I have the dinner buffet when Kim's re-opens at 7.00 pm. We do more talking than eating: a long, relaxed, easy exchange of thoughts and feelings about life's condition. We agree it is right to stay up to welcome Taymur, recognising that his '9.00 pm' might well mean 11.00 pm arrival at the hotel. I am seriously sleepy. Partway through this vigil, Eleanore gives up and goes to bed. A big party, obviously from one of the function rooms, passes through the lobby, glamorously dressed-up and radiating happiness. I stay in the lobby until 11.10 pm and then follow Eleanore's example. The next morning we discover that somehow Taymur had arrived at 10.30 pm without either of us having noticed the other: probably he came in behind the big party leaving.

Monday morning includes some other work matters: among other things, I need to speak with Edward to see if he is prepared to come with me to Kazakhstan, and wonder from whom I can get his mobile number. Then I remember that Nikki will know: the exchange of texts with her gives me a strange little frisson. Taymur takes Eleanore and me to lunch in the Avari's Japanese restaurant, where, as always, the food is good.

Eleanore worked on a project in Lahore 18 years ago but did not have much opportunity to see the principal attractions, so Taymur puts some tourism into the schedule. He has arranged for us to see the Wagha border ceremony this afternoon. I do not let Taymur know that I have seen it before: this makes me wonder to what extent the 'cultural programmes' we put on for delegations visiting London include repeat experiences.

The driver turns left outside the Avari, passing Aitchison College, which we plan to visit tomorrow. I can see it has a long red wall and a vast cricket pavilion. A flowerbed is being watered. We turn left again into Isfahan Avenue, following the canal. There are stalls selling oranges, a camel which will be used as a draught animal, and a donkey pulling a cart of tree trunks. Taymur's chatter includes various surprises. He has not seen the border ceremony before, despite having grown up in Lahore. Zain, who with his lovely cats had entertained us to dinner last year is, despite his talents, not managing his career very well. Taymur tells us that many Bollywood films are scripted in Urdu. We pass a massive street market. As we near the border, I see cows and wonder if they realise that if they walked a short distance, they could enjoy sacred status.

The road becomes dustier, and as we park, it is fog-like, with swirling miniature sandstorms. We take our seats at about 4.00 pm, on the south terrace, similarly positioned as on my previous visit. At this point, the border runs roughly north-south, and the highway from Lahore to Amritsar west-east. 'Wagha' is how the border point is spelt within Punjab; on maps produced outside that jurisdiction, it is usually 'Wagah'. To my right are the two sets of border gates, one Indian and one Pakistani, with their flags flying above. On the Pakistani side, the words 'Pakistan Zindabad' are crafted in metal, in a script that is simple Arabic rather than ornate Urdu. I comment to Eleanore, who is a more serious Arabist than me, on the Persian three dots under the first letter, converting 'B' to 'P', a sound absent from Arabic. Taymur translates 'Zindabad' as a word of general encouragement: 'Go!', or 'Long Live!' A black squirrel runs across the gate, followed by a silver one: they would know where to get the best view.

To my left is the structure which joins together the south and north terraces, forming an elaborate two-storey arch over the road, with a gallery and a castellated upper walkway: a modern structure drawing on the Moghul style, including a pair of towers with cupolas either side of a portrait of Muhammad Ali Jinnah, the father of the nation.

At 4.15 pm very loud patriotic music starts blaring out of loudspeakers, and I notice some signs of cheerleading starting on the India side. A few minutes later, one of the guards appears and marches to the border gate to liaise with his Indian opposite number. The Pakistani guards wear a black uniform, with a headdress which incorporates what I call a napkin plume because it stands up in starched pleated folds, and also a rear neck-protecting sheet which extends down the back nearly to elbow height. The sheet and plume have horizontal silver stripes through the black. The guards are exceptionally tall: that must be one of the criteria for selecting them - they peer down on the Indians. They must also be blessed with some kind of double-jointing to be able to perform high-kicks that would make the Tiller Girls jealous. Large flags are waving on the India side, where an Alsatian dog is patrolling the gate.

As 4.30 pm approaches, the terraces fill, including with a large party of hijab-wearing women, and a more complex liaison happens in 'no-man's-land' between the two sets of gates. A drummer arrives, drumming on top of frantic blaring music. The drum is of horizontal barrel shape, the skins tightly laced end to end, with many dangling tassels. It is beaten with sticks like miniature golf clubs. The Pakistani flag-waver appears. Dressed in white civilian clothing, with a flag about six feet by four feet, he trots towards the border gate with arms held out to the sides like an aeroplane, then waves the flag vigorously at the Indians, to cheering from the Pakistani benches.

At 4.40 pm, a bugle calls, and shrieked orders are followed by a drum roll, which rolls and rolls. Three guards move towards the gate, and three more come down from the high stairs of the archway, to shouts of 'Gia! Gia! Pakistan!' More guards appear, and a group of eight come under the arch and dance on the spot, forming a square. The border gate opens a fraction, briefly, and a handshake takes place between opposite sides. Guards move forward in a high arm-swinging quick march, followed by extreme high-kicks with the rear leg bent at the knee. A lot of stamping takes place, then the guards put their hands on their hips and shuffle like a bunch of ballerinas. The border gates open, and guards on both sides shake their fists at each other while slow-marching before quick-marching with arms swinging to the horizontal. The flag ropes are untied in unison. Upon orders to lower the flags, the ropes are flung in the air, partially coiled, and flung again, before being arranged into a cross, so that the two flags will pass each other in the centre of the X. Bugles play on both sides in unison (well, almost) as the flags are lowered slowly. Each side folds and carries away its flag for safe-keeping overnight. Some final high-kicks and stamping take place, the border gates close, and on the dot of 5.00 pm the spectators wander onto the parade ground.

In the minibus on the return journey, I manage to get through to Edward on the phone. Taymur is explaining the problem of Pakistan's economy, 'Of the total GDP, 40% goes on military, 40% on servicing foreign debt...', while in my other ear, Edward is coughing and sounding really unwell, but to my great relief agrees to come with me to Kazakhstan.

Back at Avari, we look at the meeting room, and unpack the boxes of materials which have arrived. Rows of pillars which will block people's view limit the options for how we can lay out the room. A man called Andrew, from Cambridge, joins us for dinner. There are four restaurants in the hotel as well as the patisserie. This evening we try out a new one which specialises in food from the Lucknow area of India. They have taken some trouble to create the ambience, including handwashing using a long-spouted jug held over a basin containing rose petals.

We deliberate over the menu: an unpleasant price one has to pay for eating in a group, and one I have never quite got used to. Why can't people just order what they themselves want to eat, and leave the sharing until later, with the foods that remain to be eaten? The starters include two kinds of kebabs: one of finely minced chicken with a slobbery texture, the other of dry, splintery lamb bones with small amounts of meat attached to them. These are served with a mint sauce, which is chilli-hot, and a papaya chutney. To follow, we have a Rogan Josh, with more bones, and a chicken curry, with a large semolina naan. We share a pudding topped with silver foil which Taymur wanted because it is one he had at home when young, but it is not the same. An after-dinner mint is served. This is stuck around with what is clearly supposed to be edible silver foil, but in fact, has a thick, tough texture like eating a chocolate one has forgotten to unwrap. Inside, the texture is wholly of betel nut, and the flavour wholly of toothpaste: overall, a seriously nasty 'treat'. The three Brits thought the meal was generally reasonable - certainly upmarket from the food which had been on offer when I visited Lucknow - but Taymur was dismissive: 'Nothing special'.

Tonight I go to bed at about 11.00 pm, setting all three alarms including the one with big bells on top. I wake at 2.30 am with a headache and thick congestion, drink water, read a while, and doze until the loud alarm rings at 4.50 am. The sky is overcast with heavy rain and continuous rumbles of thunder with lightning. I have my customary selection from the breakfast buffet, with some of a local potato dish that looks bland, but in fact is fiery and oily, then get ready to meet delegates for 7.30 am registration and 8.00 am start. After Eleanore's opening plenary, I take a group of headteachers away who have registered for a separate leadership seminar. This group includes Sarah and Tehmina. One of the inputs is a case study produced by Kiran, about a school set up by her charity. After the group have discussed the case study, Kiran and her headteacher kindly agree to join the meeting and take questions, which the group appreciate.

My seminar is finished and dispersed. I gather up the debris of my papers, feedback sheets and business cards, and decide to go to my room for 15 minutes, collecting a cup of tea on the way. Heading back to the conference area, and assuming we are about to set off on the school visit, I am surprised to meet Eleanore at the lift, heavily disguised in bathrobe and dark goggles, obviously intent on swimming. She explains that we are not now setting off until 5.50 pm. She is expecting Taymur to join her in the pool. I liaise with Taymur, who needs to repossess his laptop from the seminar room. He suggests I go to the pool. He knows I can't swim, and don't get into swimming pools, so I confirm he is meaning that it is OK for me to sit poolside.

The pool is empty except for Eleanore, swimming strongly in a cerulean blue one-piece. Trying not to distract her, I walk around the edge well back and select a chair by some trees on the far side. On the next length, she makes a gesture of acknowledgement, without losing pace. There is what sounds like a long, loud call to prayer. At 4.30 pm? It is too early for sunset. To my untutored eye, Eleanore seems to be a powerful and very fit swimmer. From my angle I see mainly the arm movements of the crawl, length after length with quick turns. Steamy vapour blows off the warm pool into the cooler air. Gusty breezes sting my eyes. A mainly leafless tree of acacia type serves as a perch for sparrows. It is behind palms and a tree that looks like a rhododendron, or perhaps a type of rubber tree. Many large kites swoop low across the pool, attracted by the warmth, or perhaps appraising Eleanore as ospreys might a salmon. I sit like Dirk Bogarde in the film *Death in Venice*, in my cream three-piece suit with red tie and handkerchief, while Eleanore pounds the water and palm fronds shiver.

Taymur arrives, wearing baggy red shorts of the kind I had myself when my daughter was little and I needed to go into water. He uses an outside shower and enters the pool on the opposite side to Eleanore. He is well-muscled and proceeds with a strong, smooth breaststroke. Nearly a hundred birds, a mixture of kites and crows, are soaring at different levels. A row of very tall, immaculate marigolds in pots stand like soldiers at one end of the pool. Finally, Eleanore is finished, climbs out, retrieves her bathrobe, and walks towards me. I go and meet her to reduce the effort required. Her goggles are off, their deep impressions remaining. I ask if she is cold, how far she has swum, and similar small-talk takes us to the lift and our separate ways, before our busy evening schedule.

We meet up in the foyer for the short drive to Aitchison College. Taymur had attended it as a student, for his sixth form education: he has not been back since, and he arranged this visit as a nostalgic indulgence. It is a boarding school set in 200 acres of parkland and playing fields, with red brick buildings in the Moghul style. Dusk has fallen as we drive into the leafy lanes of the campus towards the headquarters building. We pass the stabling for 700 ponies: necessary because the boys play polo. We have tea and biscuits with a couple of members of the senior leadership team, then set off with them to stroll around. Taymur is full of memories and questions, of course talking mainly with the staff, but occasionally pointing things out to us enthusiastically, his mind in a previous period, sharing former events, impressions and feelings with us, that in truth cannot be shared. A section of the walk takes us past one of the residential wings, where the lights inside show students reading books in their study-bedrooms and socialising in recreation rooms, in the manner of elite boarding schools worldwide.

The driver finds us and we proceed to an official reception hosted by the British Council, in the Dome Hall of the Royal Palm Golf and Country Club. The ambience and the proceedings follow the pattern for such events. A number of speeches are made, and a barbecue buffet is served on the balcony. People talk to me. Some want to know what qualifications they could take which would help them to get into the UK. One middle-aged woman tells me her life story in instalments at different points during the evening. These instalments are not sequential, as in a narrative, but adding additional layers, commencing with the formal and professional, and progressing to franker and more personal reflections on life's journey. Towards the end of the reception, I am delighted to find that Uzma is both in attendance and very willing to speak with me. I have the highest regard for Uzma's intelligence and learning, and for her professional achievements and dispositions. She is also looking even more like a film star than usual, with big bright liquid eyes, and behaving most personably. We discuss some work-related things, to be followed up by e-mails.

On Wednesday, I rejoin the main body of the conference. Delegates are giving video presentations about projects they have been undertaking under Eleanore's direction. Interesting though they are, it would be hard to maintain attention had I not been asked to act as timekeeper. During the tea break, Sarah takes the vacant seat beside me to follow up our previous conversation, and becomes trapped there by the start of the next presentation. That becomes her regular place. After the close of the formal programme, I go with Taymur, Eleanore, Kiran, the headteacher of Kiran's school, and a guide, to visit the fort and mosque, as Eleanore has not seen these sights before. This visit has to fit into a particular time slot because we are due back at the Avari later to host a poolside reception. In the event, we do not have time to go to the mosque: the women adopt a leisurely pace, talking, absorbing things, taking photographs and buying gifts. From the stalls on the approach to the main entrance to the fort, Eleanore buys gifts for her children, including a piece of sugar cane, an embroidered hat, other small items. Kiran has become a westerner for the evening, wearing jeans, a tightly waisted short jacket, and big round designer sunglasses. We buy entry tickets: £1 for foreigners, 5p for locals: a nice differential, although among our party, two of the locals are almost certainly significantly richer than the average foreign visitor.

We take the anti-clockwise route through the fort, seeing the spectacular skyline, grand ornamented pleasure courts, the Shish Mahal Mirror Palace in the north-west corner, finally proceeding down the elephant staircase. On my previous visit, its newness to me helped, I think, by having taken the clockwise route, had presented a massive 'wow' factor. Undoubtedly one of the world's 'must-sees', its scale, antiquity, clever craftsmanship and lavish ornamentation, had been deeply impressive. That is still the case, but this time I am more aware of how much is marred or missing, both through the ravages of history and shortcomings in modern custodianship.

When we are out of the fort and into the ornamental garden between it and the mosque, I get my bearings at last. Coming out of the fort, we enter the square garden in front of the mosque at one of its corners. Midway along the side to our left stands another major gateway into the fort. That gateway faces the entrance to the mosque on the opposite side of the garden. Large numbers of hooded crows swoop, peck and strut, while some of the group take photographs. Proceeding around two sides of the square garden, to the corner diagonally opposite to our entry point, we go out through a heavy gateway which I have not seen or explored previously. This leads into the street containing Cooco's Den, which I later discover is now called Food Street. The gateway connects two memorable panoramas: the pieces of the jigsaw now fall into place. Back through the gate into the garden, we complete the other two sides of the square, pass the entrance to the mosque but agree we have insufficient time for a visit. The place where the car is parked is full of dust clouds and rickshaws.

When we work with Taymur's organisation in Karachi, the commander throws a party in his house, providing wonderful hospitality: food, alcoholic drink, and the cream of Karachi society. Here in Lahore, Taymur has organised a modest drinks reception at the poolside in the Avari, which, like the commander's parties, is for guests only, not for conference delegates. Taymur does not touch alcohol himself, and I wonder about the logistical difficulties he must have gone through to set up this event in a 'dry' country. This is the event we needed to get back to. On the way back, near to the hotel, someone suggests we pull up alongside the Chumman ice cream shop. In the event, there is only one taker, but while this transaction is ongoing, street traders poke various tacky toys through the window for inspection.

The hotel staff have set up the bar, chairs, low tables, candles, bowls of nuts and other nibbles to create a pleasant evening ambience. Eleanore's friend Hek is in attendance, smoking heavily as always, and drinking heavily to make good use of the opportunity. I drink a few glasses of cool white wine, which is pleasant and relaxing, but despite my good relationship with alcohol, in truth I would feel more comfortable not touching it while being a guest in a Muslim country. A conversation starts between myself and a woman working in Lahore with one of the UK organisations. Because both of us need to be seen to be talking to someone: that is the polite thing to do. After a few minutes, she realises I have worked with the same bits of government, and on the same issues as her and the polite exchange graduates into a mutually interesting and enjoyable professional dialogue.

After the reception has dispersed, Eleanore and I need to plan the arrangements for group presentations the following day, which we do in the hotel foyer, helped by peppermint tea and a chicken croissant. I go to my room at 11.40 pm, but need to do some work on flight options for Kazakhstan, and get to bed at 1.00 am. On Thursday, I am up at 5.30 am to allow time for some practical preparations for the group presentations. These duly take place quite smoothly, notwithstanding that six groups have to work in the same room with only one projector between them. In the spaces, we try to check-in online, which is just as well, really, because we find that Eleanore's booking has disappeared. This occasions a great deal of faffing around, involving Taymur's excellent IT skills and the advice of his local travel agent. In the end, the only solution is to sit out the time difference until our project administrator in London is on duty, and get him on to the booking agent who finds that the booking reference for Eleanore had been changed. This is odd, because it is a return ticket and the flight out had worked without problem.

Sarah has dispensed with her gloves. Her hands are slender and golden, with coloured nails. During the afternoon, I get her talking about herself, and she explains that she adopted the hijab after going on pilgrimage. The experience had deeply impressed her, and she had taken up her style of dress as part of that spiritual milestone. I listen with interest; she goes on to the rationale that she does not wish to be objectified as a woman, preferring people to get to know her as a person before forming judgements. I understand and respected that standpoint, but feel we have established sufficient rapport for me to suggest that dealing with objectification may not be that simple. In a gentle way, I put forward the possibility that if a man finds a woman attractive, her wearing a hijab may not entirely eradicate that sentiment, and might even strengthen it. The attraction may be based on a different set of factors to those that apply to a young woman dressed for clubbing on a Friday night, but some men would find the fully covered style alluring, graceful and feminine. Whatever the words I actually used, she seems to take them as a compliment.

At about 4.15 pm, after the certificates have been handed out, and the group photographs taken, and most of the farewells conducted, I sit tidying up a mess of disarranged working papers, selecting those I want from those that can be binned, while enjoying the sense of completion – a kind of pleasurable exhaustion: permission to relax, no longer on show and on duty - which comes at the end of any assignment. Sarah and I exchange compliments and arrangements to keep in touch: of course, a contactless parting. There have been some options offered to us for early evening activity between this point and departing at 7.30 pm for dinner in the old town. These include going to the traditional cultural crafts centre run by Taymur's sister, and going to Taymur's mother's fashion stall. We take the decision that rest and relaxation are a more welcome use of the time. Kiran invites me, then Eleanore, to go shopping in the clothes market: we refuse.

In my room, I e-mail home and sort out flights to Kazakhstan, whilst drinking two cups of tea, and then enjoy the remaining hour mainly reading a novel, having decided there is insufficient time to sleep. At 7.00 pm I go to Taymur's room where Eleanore and Hek are already gathered for the purpose of drinking some of the alcohol left over from the poolside party. Heck proves efficacious at this: in the end, I don't think much has to be poured down the drain. Then the dinner party assembles in the lobby, its additional members being the female head of an American international school and two Sudanese staff of a Saudi school. The seven of us set off for the old town in two cars.

Turning right out of the Avari, which involves going left some way first, we head into an area of traffic congestion, not helped by a number of donkey carts. Animated people in happy evening mood sway past on motorbikes. We pass the State Bank, styled like a cathedral, the Lahore Museum, and Government College. When we get to the old town, the driver goes down Food Street and deposits us at the Fort View Restaurant, right on the corner opposite the gate into the garden and fort.

The restaurant displays for sale a great array of contemporary figurative art, depictions of human forms which, to say the least, are not demur in style. Our table is on the open-air top floor. Some take the spiral stairs; I take the lift. From our corner vantage point, the flood-lit mosque is spectacular in its beautiful proportions against the inky sky. Drums play loudly in the street below, while the restaurant's loudspeakers broadcast Eastern-style pop music. Lighting, mainly from candles, is minimal. This adds an element of groping and mystery to the eating process. I am sitting opposite the Sudanese men, and the combination of music, drumming, open air, their soft voices and accents, and my deafness, severely restrict meaningful conversation. In this sensorially impaired fashion, I enjoy the starter of salads, with spicy dips, and raita reassuringly served in sealed Nestle tubs with use-by dates. Kebabs follow, of reasonable quality and vast quantity: lamb, fish, chicken, with rice and naan. The meal finishes with a wonderful tray of sweets, including sugar-coated fennel seeds, small soft aniseed balls, and similar delights. While enjoying them, I wonder how many people's dirty fingers had been poking around in them.

After the meal, we wander along Food Street. Hek walks in a different direction, where I believe there may be a place of adult entertainment. I look into Cooco's Den, but the arrangement of the buildings has changed: it is all completely different. The street itself is different. It has been cleaned up, and the buildings are brightly lit, with more cafes. The street has been prettified for tourists, including horse and cart rides, a decorated bus, fancy lighting. It has lost the character I had found attractive on my previous visit. The party is strung out, and wandering along on my own towards where the cars are parked, I feel completely safe and relaxed: perhaps that is a positive effect of the changes.

When we get back to the hotel, a member of staff has packages for us. Kiran has bought us clothes in the market: for me, a patterned Shalwar Kameez and white trousers. Later we meet in the foyer lounge for tea. Hek appears to have found, in the meantime, a source of alcohol: he is garrulous, satirical, argumentative. He decides he is hungry and fancies some Chinese food. The hotel has an excellent Chinese restaurant, but he doesn't want to leave the lounge. He argues, first with us and then with a nonplussed member of staff, that it is a reasonable request for someone to bring him something from the Chinese restaurant to where he is sitting. Eventually, with bad grace, he accepts the offer of a club sandwich as an alternative form of blotting paper.

On Friday morning, my alarm at 5.00 am coincides with the morning call to prayer. We set off for the airport at 6.30 am. The flight to Dubai is marked by prolonged heavy turbulence: about the most dramatic I can recall. At Dubai we have plenty of time to go to Oberjin. Eleanore's stomach is not perfect: she thinks Chardonnay might help. She is on the phone to her colleague in Egypt, who, in the event has changed plans and is no longer able to meet in person. The phone call goes on a bit so I order my food and Eleanore's drink. I choose salmon fillet, provencal tomatoes, green salad, Bearnaise sauce, and breads and butters. The waiter cannot believe how much liquid I want to go with that: Chardonnay, watermelon juice and a pot of Lapsang Souchong. 'We are thirsty', I explain. All of these items are excellent, and Eleanore passes me most of her Chardonnay. She judges her phone conversation excellent also, so we are both happy.

Chapter Fourteen

Astana: First Steppe, Last Step

I know as I set off that this will be the final step, or, as it happens, steppe, of the journey which with this book is concerned. This gives a reflective quality to my preparations, and to the train ride south on Saturday 29 March 2014. I seized the opportunity to squeeze in this final assignment, bringing as it does the chance to see a new country: Kazakhstan. Country number 20 since this adventure began in 2007; trip number 49: five continents spanned. I will get back on Thursday 3 April, when I will go into the office to tie up loose ends: I finish this employment a couple of days later.

A one-way ticket to Astana, via Almaty, arrived a few days ago. I joked with colleagues about this apparently deliberate parting gift. Information about the hotel and pick-up arrangements followed shortly afterwards. Early on Thursday afternoon, I packed as many of my personal papers as I could carry, left my office for good and went home. On Friday, e-tickets for the return journey arrived, and I was told passports with visas had been returned to the agency. Edward kindly agreed to pick mine up with his, although I dislike the lack of independence. Edward would also be the courier for the signed contract for the work we will be doing: 'just-in-time' management to the very last.

These developments enable the formalities for insurance and permission to travel to be dashed off.

It is always slightly worrying travelling from Barnard Castle to Heathrow on the same day as the flight: there are too many things that could go wrong. The ticketing website has not let me book onto the 8.30 am train, telling me it is full, which I do not believe, so I am on the much slower 8.57 am stopping service. I am in time to watch the 8.30 am come in, pulled by the diesel named Flying Scotsman: in fairness, it does seem fully ticketed. My train south is bedevilled with minor difficulties: trespassers on the line, a faulty level crossing, being stuck behind a slow train, and so on. At King's Cross, hurrying to the Piccadilly Line, I notice by chance rather than design that there are engineering works on the way to Heathrow, involving major delays and alternative bus services. Feeling relieved not to have made a bad mistake, I opt for the extravagant but more certain choice of the Heathrow Express, and arrive at Terminal 4 in good time.

Edward is neither present nor contactable, so at about 1.45 pm I pick Café Rouge as the place to sit, with a peppermint tea and a late breakfast which includes black pudding. At about 2.45 pm I make contact with Edward: he has got caught up in the engineering works and is on his way in a taxi. We check in at about 3.15 pm: it is a relief to be reunited with passport and visa. Earlier, check-in had been empty, but now it is crowded with people showing that characteristic check-in demeanour of tedium and drudgery. Through in departures, I have tea in Dining Street (a play on Downing Street) and buy Fisherman's Friends and a bottle of Lipton's Tea (peach flavoured variety) from Boots, while Edward does other things, including charging up his laptop.

Kazakhs I have met previously in work contacts have been mainly of the northern, Russian kind. I am interested to see that at the boarding gate, most of the passengers are East Asian, and when we board, the cabin crew are universally so. The plane is a smallish Boeing 757, with a central aisle and three leather seats on either side. The flight is packed with too much hand baggage: cases are stuffed into every corner, and some tumble to the floor on take-off, which was supposed to have been at 5.15 pm but is an hour late. The meal is good: both choices equally appetising and nicely served. I set my watch straightaway to Almaty time: six hours ahead, but probably only five, as British Summer Time starts during the flight. TV screens are suspended from the central aisle, and the nearest is some distance away. At 2.45 am, I notice that we have passed to the north of Kiev and are just about to pass to the south of Moscow. A small, fiddly immigration form is given out: trying to fill it in sets off a small-scale migraine aura, which I take as a sign that it is time to dim the light and try to rest. Actually my aisle seat, which I had asked for, is right next to the toilets, where the light stays on, and people and machinery are noisy.

The plane descends over Almaty, a sprawling city, to the airport among grassy fields on its far side. Emerging from the plane, there are rugged, snow-topped mountains to the south: my first view of the Himalayas from the northern side. Edward has disembarked well ahead of me: he had not been fully well when we set off and he has passed an uncomfortable night. The passport queue I join is held up a while, and it is not very clear where to go. I come out of arrivals, to be accosted by offers of taxis, and eventually find that I need to go upstairs to find domestic departures. One of those accosting me is hard to shake off. I buy some local currency, because my guide book implies that traders and hotels are no longer supposed to accept US Dollars. The money-changer does not have much English. She rejects my $100 note. She holds up a new, perfect one, and points to the slight crease across one corner of mine. 'You think not good?', I persist, passing it back again, aware that none of my much-travelled USD are going to be pristine. Memories of Yemen, and a bank quite prepared to reject the dollars which it itself issued from its own cash machine. The transaction proceeds, and for my creased $100 note I received 18,000 bright, colourful somethings: the name of the unit of currency is only in Cyrillic script.

Through security at last into the small and not well-equipped departures area, Edward hails me and discusses buying tea, using some of his own USD here, which should be possible. I accept this kind gesture, and when the tea comes it is of that same mellow, non-acrid type I had enjoyed on the plane, which reminds me of a leaf-tea I used to buy called Russian Caravan. Edward sits separately, with his laptop open, working on a book. I admire his application. He explains that he must provide chapters for this one by Thursday. Edward is a prolific writer of academic books, and he says that they generate about £10,000 in royalties for him each year. With only minor interruptions, he perseveres with the work during the next leg of the flight.

The plane is of the same kind as before, and as before, lemon-flavoured boiled sweets are issued for take-off and landing. I doze on the flight while Edward bends over his laptop, refining text. A hot pasty is served, filled with vegetables and, I think, chicken, which with tomato juice, nice black tea, and a Bounty bar whose wrapper was adorned with some Cyrillic script, makes a welcome snack. The ethnic profile of passengers on this internal flight is more mixed. While still quite a few have East Asian features, some have more South Asian characteristics, reminding me of people from the north of Pakistan. Others are more Russian type.

At Astana airport, we are picked up quickly in a Toyota saloon with dark-shaded rear windows. Driving on the right, and smelling strongly of tobacco, the driver takes us on a wide, dead-straight road across flat steppe, with brown grass, snowy patches, and brown bare trees: lines of fir beside the road, and stands of silver birches further back. Settlements come into view: blocks under construction, looking drab and old before they are even finished, and among trees and on wasteground, many shacks. No other word describes them: of various constructions and colour, but all of the same simple rectangular shape, with a window set high in the end wall, so single storey but with an attic room under the eaves.

Of my road passenger experiences in different countries in recent times, this is by far the most sedate: never faster than 90 Km/h and with traffic lights and junctions treated with chauffer-style respect. We come to the capital city, with much new buildings and many construction sites. There are two stadia styled like the Millennium Dome, a conventional football ground, another sports stadium, and an enormous 'Fitness Palace'.

The buildings are in a range of dramatic styles. Cylindrical tower blocks seem to be popular. Further away, I see a tower block with a rectangular section but inverse perspective, so it grows wider towards the top like a skyscraper in a cartoon. An enormous development is in the form of turrets with an arch between them. Another is shaped like a Greek temple. One mountainous pile of apparently residential development is covered with a forest of thin, spiky towers, which made me think of Milan Cathedral with its hair standing on end. Another building takes the form of chunky round towers, capped with cone-shaped roofs, each topped with a tall, cylindrical spire like a chimney, an overall effect slightly reminiscent of Battersea Power Station. We pass the Cardiac Surgery Research Centre, cross the mighty river, see a Radisson Hotel, and a Park Inn; we turn right, then left, stop quite abruptly, and suddenly we have arrived.

When we get out, the sign does indeed say 'Grand Park Esil' (there are various transliterations: it is sometimes written as 'Yessil'). In her note, Dina had said, 'This is the hotel you will be staying at – it is in the heart of the old city, right bank of the Ishim River'. My guide book's description of the hotel, read in conjunction with a street plan, make it sound as if it is near a great park and interesting buildings. On greater investigation, that may all be true, but at first sight it is hard to equate those expectations to the nondescript urban scene in front of me. The check-in clerk cannot find any reservations for us. On reflection, I realise I have never seen them myself, but we persist and are admitted. It is, by now, about 10.30 am and Edward makes clear his intention to rest. I survey my room's not very generous comforts, check the vital matter of e-mail connectivity, and sleep for a couple of hours.

The shower cubicle has minimal floor area, but compensates with ridiculous height, reflecting the city's architecture. Outside this construction, a quite substantial glass corner-shelf unit is fixed so high that I have to stretch to inspect its minimal contents. A tiny rectangle of cheap soap partially wrapped in a thin strip of paper, and a tiny bottle of 'sampoo+hair kream' which, when I use it, feels as if it is the same soap merely diluted. This seems to be an insufficient array to justify the shelves. There is no kettle in the room.

Bravely, prompted by a need for tea, I explore. Out of a window on the landing in one direction is an enormous branch of Burger King.

Further along, in another direction, is a view of various new roofs, covered in lumpy old snow, including what might have been a grander entrance to this hotel. Having examined information in the room, I head to the lobby bar. This is supposed to be open, but it is deserted. I am told to wait. Two waitresses come to attend to my needs, but after giving my order, I am directed to the Polo Restaurant, whence they had evidently come.

For ease of communication, I had asked for tea and a club sandwich, not something I would normally choose, having seen this item described in the room service menu. I had already peeped into the Polo Restaurant, which was also deserted (at 3.00 pm on a Sunday?) but had decided it was too posh for my current needs. Nevertheless, back I am by direction. I notice the restaurant sign in Russian script, which looks similar to 'pectopah' and remember being told that English people want to say 'pectopah', whereas if they just said 'restaurant' that would be quite near to the transliteration. The manager is a fair European, the staff East Asian. The one who serves me is slender, gentle and smiling. She brings a substantial teapot with two tags of Lipton's Yellow Label hanging out of it, sets it down prettily, and nervously offers to pour, which makes me feel that suddenly bright sunlight is streaming into the room.

Background music includes a Tchaikovsky ballet. Oil paintings of limited artistic merit depict the Eiffel Tower and the Moulin Rouge. The club sandwich appears next, presented exactly as the one which had been the subject of Hek's drunken remonstrations in the Avari. Clearly, this is How It Is Done. A large square plate, with a pile of hot chips in the middle, and quarters of the sandwich arranged in each corner, their double-decker structure held together with cocktail sticks. I am surprised to find that the sandwich, while made of toast, is chill-cold. I remember the description: 'roasted toast, with boiled chicken, and boiled egg': true enough. It also includes good pickled cucumbers. A knife and fork seem the only practical way to proceed, which means deconstructing the sandwich because the 'roasted toast' requires quite firm hacking.

My guide book says that it is polite in Kazakhstan to eat with loud lip-smacking of food, vigorous slurping of tea, and resonant belching: that such signs of appreciation will engender warm acceptance and make everyone happy. I wonder if sometimes the writers of guides play a bit of a joke on the trusting, well-meaning traveller, and decide not to risk deliberate amplification. My unintentional signs of appreciation probably convey sufficient goodwill.

I wander into the lobby, where settees are placed around a beautiful, large carpet of central Asian geometric design. The predominant colour is between a dark salmon pink and a faded terracotta, against a background of muted blue-grey and beige. I browse a three-day-old copy of the (English language) *Astana Times*. This tells stories of booming economic development and mineral exploitation, combined with nature preservation and a lot of culture. Someone with the same surname as our host is being featured for her promotion of English language teaching. An art exhibition by Viktor Kell, a Kazakh resident in Astana, is well covered, with illustrations of bold modern portraits, although the exhibition also includes 50 watercolours of 'Winter in Astana'. He has a brother, Vyacheslev Kell, who is also an artist, and they have recently done a joint exhibition in Crimea of Crimean scenes. A Kazakhstani film based on Hemingway's *Old Man and The Sea* has been nominated for an award. There is news of the opera, and of a Kazakh ship delivering grain to Iran across the Caspian Sea, that exotic waterway bringing to my mind a picture of a Quinquereme of Nineveh, and some lines from the poem 'Sohrab and Rustum'.

On Monday morning, refreshed by a good sleep, I explore the breakfast offerings in the Polo Restaurant and spot Edward in the farthest corner with a book open, so I choose a table nearby within conversational range, but not so close as to restrict his options. For breakfast I enjoy borscht, in which the main ingredient is cabbage, and a mixed platter of warm potatoes sprinkled with parsley, warm tomato, and warm meat borek – the region's answer to toad in the hole. But I do not enjoy a chill-cold runny fried egg: a revolting combination of temperature and texture.

Peeter meets us in the lobby and we start the minibus ride to the venue. The driver wears a Mao-style cap. His seat back and headrest are covered with a thick sheepskin. The many trees edging the streets have the bottom few feet of their trunks painted white: a form of protection against pests that I associate with hot countries and am surprised to see here among patches of snow, then I remember that the summers will be as hot as in the tropics. The streets form a grid pattern and include wide boulevards. Peeter starts a helpful running commentary. He is a much-travelled Estonian: a seasoned consultant who knows Astana well and has helped us to get this assignment. He is a specialist in bi- and multi-lingualism, and for him, Kazakhstan offers a rare case study of tri-lingual education, as books and teaching use Russian, Kazakh and English in more or less equal measures.

Peeter explains that ethnic Kazakhs now made up about 63% of the population of Kazakhstan, having fallen to about 39% in Stalin's time. Ethnic Kazakhs have features which can range from Turkish to Chinese in appearance. Astana's population has grown by 80% since 2009. Traffic is busy, and this enables me to get a better look than yesterday at some of the buildings. Peeter points out one of several buildings designed by Norman Foster, which is conical and surmounted by a leaning pole. We pass a steam bath in a grand building in the style of an eastern palace, like the shapes across the front of some boxes of Turkish delight. Next is a row of restaurants built in various styles of imitation. One is copying the style of old Uzbekistan; another is a large wooden windmill. I learn that the building shaped like a Greek temple is the opera house. Peeter explains how certain buildings are lined up, so that from the Norman Foster building, the golden eagle-egg tower could be seen through the enormous arch of one of the government buildings.

The streets are extravagantly ornamented. There are large glass tulips which light up, many tree lights, and a full-size group of horses cantering towards the road, made out of a shiny ceramic material.

The venue is a school, which also serves as the headquarters of a chain of similarly prestigious, highly resourced schools for specially selected students of high academic ability. Although relatively new, and by most standards well-equipped (except for the row of squats with non-fastening doors in the students' toilets), this building is to be replaced by a better one, which is currently under construction. Dina finds us and introduces herself: she is the person in the client organisation who has made all the arrangements.

The room for the event is a large theatre with steeply tiered seats in a straight line, and a floor space between these and a stage. On the seats are 90 people: 30 from the Ministry, and the remainder from several of the Ministry's significant national agencies. They are to receive five days of inputs from various visiting experts, then split into three groups for a further five days. All materials are in three languages, with simultaneous translation throughout. The programme says that there will be quite a few formal introductory speeches from senior politicians and officials. In fact, these are fewer and shorter, which means that Peeter, the expert for Day 1, has rather more of the day to fill than he had anticipated.

Mid-morning and mid-afternoon, there are breaks with refreshments, which for visiting speakers and organising officials are served in a room laid out for about twenty people, separately from the participants who mill around in halls and corridors. The refreshments include green or black tea and substantial pastries: a particularly popular kind is filled with cold cooked cabbage. These pastries are also on the table as an extra filler at lunch, which is waitress-served more formally in the same room. On the first day, lunch starts with borscht, which is mainly cabbage. This is followed by a burger with sticky rice, with a side dish of carrot and cucumber salad containing fish, and a soft drink made out of dried fruit.

Language barriers limit conversation with our hosts apart from those with designated liaison duties. The senior officials of the host organisation are evidently proud of what they are doing, and strongly self-assured about its rightness and the certainty of successful outcomes. They have extensive powers to make people do things, ample government money, and presidential approval, and their eyes, body language and the deference of their juniors attest those qualities. We talk quite a bit with representatives of another UK agency which has a long-term involvement in the project, more substantial than ours.

When the programme has finished for the day, Dina takes Edward and me to Nazarbayev University. We leave the venue by a back door and the driver takes us across a muddy, rutted building site edged with silver birches, into a part of the city where Dina points out a velodrome and a skating rink. There is an area of scrubland with shacks similar to those I had noticed coming from the airport, and Dina explains that these are holiday homes: these ones near the city centre pre-date the growth of Astana.

Somehow the topic of borders arises, and Dina says that there is usually little formality within the free trade area with Russia and Belarus. Some train rides cross borders and back again in the course of the journey: occasionally, an official might get on the train during one of these incursions and make an issue about passengers crossing the border without proper papers.

As we approach the university campus, Dina points out a large building being constructed of a brick-red material: this is the new school to replace the one serving as our current venue. The university, one of the many prestigious constructions bearing the president's name, is massively impressive. The foyer opens into a spacious mall with sufficient water features and shiny marble to satiate a Middle Eastern prince. Hardly anyone is around. We meet a person attached to Dina's organisation who is in charge of leadership development programmes for headteachers. For an hour or so we have a pleasant, professional conversation. Dina stays to do further work with her colleague; Edward and I are driven back to our hotel.

Earlier in the day, Peeter had very kindly said that he wanted to give us the experience of a 'cheap and cheerful' real Kazakh restaurant with which he was familiar. We meet in the lobby at the agreed time, and he leads us from the hotel in what must be a southerly direction. It is dark but bright from street lamps, fairy lights, neon signs, and illuminated street sculptures. Our walk brings us to a kind of pedestrian viewing area on the bank of the river, which I now understand is called Ishim in Russian and Esil in Kazakh. We are on its north bank: its right bank, as it is flowing from left to right from our vantage point, but this is not obvious because it is still almost entirely frozen, with snow piled on the ice. The river flows north, and after various confluences, becomes the Ob which flows into the Arctic Ocean. It is much wider than the Thames, and we are looking across to the Central Park on the south bank. Both banks are lit up in a way reminiscent of the Lumiere light show in Durham. In addition to fixed lights of every kind and colour, moving light shows are projected onto a number of the tall buildings.

Peeter tells us the restaurant is nearby, and leads us across the road to a large, heavy door. This separates the quiet, cold, spacious, concrete, glass and neon world outside, from the hot, crowded, noisy, timber and fabric world inside the restaurant. Peeter had warned, 'They will *insist* on taking your coats' - he seemed to have an issue, or perhaps a bad experience, regarding parting with outerwear. This essential ritual is performed in a vestibule closed in with heavy carved wooden beams and panels. That aspect of decor continues into the body of the restaurant, where it is relieved by brilliant fabrics of rainbow-coloured geometric Central Asian design: cushions, draperies, pelmets.

Alcoholic drink is allowed only in the section of the restaurant nearest the door, which is packed. Peeter establishes that there is no possibility of seating in the near future, so we reluctantly move through to the much larger area, which is less ornamented and has more of the feel of a place for families. We are chased by a member of staff who explains in Kazakh and gestures that we can, after all, be accommodated in the drinking area, a party having just left. He guides us to a large table surrounded by cushioned bench seats, enclosed in a wooden compartment with draperies, almost like dining inside a four-poster bed.

The staff and the clientele (except ourselves) are all Chinese-featured Kazakhs. Most of the clientele are animated young groups and couples enjoying themselves, many wearing items of clothing in ethnic fabrics similar to the cushions. Peeter is our spokesperson: I am not sure, amongst the bustle and with my limited linguistic knowledge, whether he is conversing in Russian or Kazakh. He establishes that there is no menu in English. We ask him to choose for us, and he orders beer, bread, and a tasty soup with filled dumplings similar to ravioli.

As we are walking back from the restaurant, and I am thinking what a relaxed and safe environment it is, I notice a car, on the pavement, advancing towards us at at least 40 mph, with dazzling main beam headlamps. I am walking on the outside, most directly exposed to this threat, but also best placed to evaluate it. As soon as I see it, I estimate that it will probably miss us by an inch or two. Reluctantly I step about four inches to the left and am glad to have done so. The others react less phlegmatically.

On Tuesday, I am up early, having set the alarm for 5.00 am. I shower and look through the presentations I will be giving. Breakfast is not quite so good as on the first morning: weird pastry things and bland, not very hot, lentil soup. Edward is not at all well: he struggles through the day. We are picked up by the minibus and taken to the school. It is colder, with quite a nip in the air, although the locals explain that they find it sweltering because it is not -40C. They say that in the cold season, when it gets to -30C the schools are shut to children but the staff still have to go in, until it gets to -40C. Then in the summer, it is often around +35C or hotter.

The scheduling for the day is already fairly tight, but a woman in a senior position decides to give a lecture of at least 45 minutes about a project she is doing, in time which had been allocated to us, without any discussion or notice. After that, I start my first input and do about half of what I planned. Then tea break happens, after which Edward does his first input, but overruns, so then it is lunchtime. This is served in the usual room, and consists of cabbage soup with chicken, followed by fine slivers of tough meat cooked in a creamy sauce, with very sloppy mashed potato, and a side dish of coleslaw. The cold, cabbage-filled pastries continue to add to the items on the table. Clearly cabbages are plentiful around here. Lunch is accompanied by a pink-coloured soft drink made from corn syrup. It is a long break because the participants are transported to a ministry building for their lunch, so I get given a guided tour of the school library.

Edward presents his second input after lunch and mercifully truncates it. I do a quick one, then have to make space for a teacher to give a presentation promoting the use of a particular ICT software package. After afternoon tea, I give two more presentations in succession and finish with an open forum which goes smoothly enough, although it became apparent yesterday day that most of the participants are inhibited from saying anything in front of the ministry officials. The inhibition is understandable, as we are told that when one participant expresses an opinion, the murmurs around them are Kazhak for 'Shut up'. Clearly, the situation here conforms to a model which crops up here and there around the world. A dictator with a tight grip on the nation, and unfettered access to the nation's considerable wealth, is imposing a new education system, and the professionals who must deliver the change are not to have any opinions about it. And here we are, thinking that education enables people to make informed choices, to take ownership of their lives. We won't be asked back, that's for sure.

After the end of the day, which has included some contractual formalities – I will need to call in at the office on my return to deliver signed documents for countersigning - there is a sightseeing tour. I set off with Dina, Peeter and Edward, who nobly bears it so as not to prevent the activity. Peeter had previously said, 'This is not a walkable city: the buildings are so huge that you think they are nearer than they are.' I get in the minibus and start a migraine aura: this is on cue, I'd been expecting it, having completed the formal part of my work. So, like Edward, I am not exactly the most enthusiastic sightseer. I do, nevertheless, see lots of amazing buildings, all in different very striking styles, on a big scale: the sort of mixture of opulent tastes which make me think of Riyadh and Dubai. In fact, I learnt that Astana has close links with the Middle East. I see towers, including ones covered with gold-tinted glass; parliament, ministries, and the President's headquarters. In caring old Soviet style there are lines of buses waiting to take all the government workers home. Because they work long hours, there are more buses arranged all through the evening. As it is a new capital, a big proportion of the population work for government agencies.

We follow the grand promenade from the ministries to the golden bird's-egg tower. Peeter and Dina explain that this is an exhibition centre, with a central lift up to the inside of the orb, from which spectacular views may be seen. Flurries of snow are falling. We enter the ground floor of the tower. 'They will *insist* on taking your coats', Peeter warns, but in the event, the cloakroom and ticket booth are unstaffed for a period and we decide not to wait. By this time, the traffic has become very thick, so I have an extended chat with Dina on the way back to the hotel. During this drive, we pass a group of colourful yurts pitched by the roadside. I wonder whether this is a folk museum exhibit, but no, Dina says it is quite normal: a group of yurt-dwelling people are visiting the town.

David wants to rest straight away; I dine alone in the hotel. I feel quite hungry and want to comfort-eat as a way of relaxing. I have a pot of tea at the start of the meal, a starter of Russian herring with pickled cucumber, followed by baked salmon with chips, and look at a fresh *Times* crossword that I have kept for the occasion.

For Wednesday morning, we have arranged to go back to the school to watch a couple of lessons. The soup at breakfast continues to deteriorate: this one is white, sour, and cheesy, flecked with mint. I follow this with various warm savoury pastries, and a warm tomato, followed in turn (not knowing what would be happening about lunch) by a cold platter of beef sausage, olives, cucumber, and tinned pear.

Edward and I sit in the minibus quite a while. The driver, in Russian and by holding up four fingers and pointing to his watch, explains our lack of movement. Two other passengers arrive: when we speak with them, going into the school, we learn that they are from Denmark and are presenting today's programme. We are taken to meet the principal, who speaks to us through an interpreter. Then we watch two lessons: one on ICT, the other on English language. In both cases, the class consists of ten students, with two teachers. I assume this generous staffing is to ensure that between them, the teachers are fluent in all three languages, to uphold the school's trilingual policy. But the students are docile, and the teaching and learning activities are undemanding, so the class could be twice the size without any loss of quality.

Edward had previously mentioned a couple of times that he is anxious to send someone a postcard but has not found the means to do so. This is now becoming a more urgent desire. Back at the hotel, we explore what looks like a shop but isn't. Edward asks the receptionist, who seems quite vague about what is wanted, but says she will order a stamp. Edward is not convinced that he wants any lunch, but I point out that it will be a long time until we are fed on the flight, and he joins me in the Polo Restaurant. I pick the set lunch of rough, garlicky meatballs and cold, sloppy, white spaghetti, which is a disappointing experience, and two pots of tea. Edward has soup, lager and coffee.

The receptionist directs Edward to a bookshop which will sell postcards. I say I will go with him. We walk around three sides of a block:

I enjoy the opportunity to get a taste of the street scene in daylight. The bookshop is interesting, but its single member of staff does not understand what a postcard is. After various attempts at communication, a customer helpfully interprets. When the shop assistant understands what a postcard is, she confirms that they don't have any. Back at the hotel, the receptionist suggests trying the Post Office. Another pleasant short walk to this promising destination takes place. It is entirely devoted to very official-looking business at various booths and counters, except for a newsagent's stall which does not sell postcards. Back at the hotel, the receptionist reports that the stamp she had ordered has not been sent.

We work in our rooms until 5.00 pm, then wait in the lobby until the taxi comes for us at 5.30 pm. Checking out of the hotel is unproblematical: I part with some pretty-coloured notes, but the main bill has been met by the Ministry. We find the airport initially confusing: we wander upstairs, downstairs, to left and right, trying to work out the procedure for international departure. This confusion resolves itself into simplicity, and suddenly we are through into the departure area with the shortest and easiest procedure either of us can remember. It is a small airport, with limited facilities. Edward still hopes for a postcard: we amble round the one shop, but among the perfumes and gifts, none is to be found. I hope for tea. We pass the entrance to a paid-for lounge offering all manner of luxuries which we don't feel are necessary. At the end of the long, narrow departure area is a cafe. Edward wants only tea; I buy a square of honey cake to have with mine. While doing this transaction, I notice Edward has chosen a seat in a faraway corner rather than in the cafe and has his laptop open. I carry over his tea, meaning to return for mine, but the man from the cafe kindly follows.

The choice of flights between London and Kazakhstan, on the one Kazakh airline considered safe enough to be allowed into EU airspace, is quite limited, and for our return journey, the Ministry has booked us to fly from Astana to Abu Dhabi, thence to Heathrow. This roundabout route, heading south instead of north, taking the other two sides of a triangle rather than the hypotenuse, adds at least three hours of actual flight time.

We have three hours at Abu Dhabi between landing and take-off.

After moving through the transit area, that leaves the best part of two hours to fill before boarding. Since neither of us is interested in shopping, we find a table in the food court. Edward will take only tea; I choose a sort of roll filled with chicken and salad to go with mine. The air is, of course, quite warm, and many of the people milling about are lightly clad in holiday mode. By contrast, having chosen my single travelling outfit for a cold country, I am wearing a four-piece Harris Tweed suit with matching cap. I take off the cap and overcoat and convince myself that by sitting still, the open weave of the fabric will keep me from sweltering.

An array of flight information screens are within reading distance of our table. Our flight, at 2.35 am, is not yet showing, which is indicative of the huge volume of traffic. Compulsively, I keep looking at it, especially when new flights are added, and all the information reshuffles position, waiting the long seconds for the display to flick from Arabic to English.

Edward has his computer open and corrects text between conversations. When he goes to the bathroom and asks me to look after his things, 'So you don't want me to press "delete"?' I joke. Because he is earnest, diligent and strongly principled, I have come to realise that one way to entertain Edward is for me to behave slightly Puckishly and to pretend to hold whacky political stances. In this way, conversation flows sufficiently. When he realises I am going into the office the following morning, straight off the flight, in order to deliver the signed contract, he is alarmed and urges me not to tell anyone he is back. I am well familiar with the issues of fending off demands on the day following a night flight, and it is relaxing to think that this is unlikely to be a problem for me in the future.

The screen flickers; the new flights added are creeping nearer to the time for ours. I ponder ways in which I had developed, and ways in which I had stayed the same, through the events of the last seven years, remembering successes and shortcomings, as people and places swirl through my mind. The screen changes again and announces the flight that will take me to the end of this journey and the start of a different one.

Also by Raphael Wilkins

Accidental Traveller

An Educational Journey

Policy Transfer & Educational Change

*Education in the Balance: Mapping the Global Dynamics
of School Leadership*

Printed in Great Britain
by Amazon